Holy Wow!

Holy Wow!

The Blessing Is Being Here

Volume I

Dana St. Claire

© 2020 by Maylaigh Media

All rights reserved. No part of this book may be reproduced or transmitted in any form or by any means, electronic or mechanical, including photocopying, recording, or by any information storage and retrieval system, except in the case of brief quotations embodied in critical articles and reviews, without prior written permission of the publisher.

Although the author and publisher have made every effort to ensure the accuracy and completeness of information contained in this book, we assume no responsibility for errors, inaccuracies, omissions, or any inconsistency herein.

ISBN Paperback: 978-1-7331059-0-3
ISBN eBook: 978-1-7331059-2-7
ISBN Audio: 978-1-7331059-1-0

Cover artwork: Miladinka Milic
Interior design: Ghislain Viau

I dedicate this book to my remarkable daughter, Lyla.
My role model for embracing Life.
Thanks, Darlin', for ALL your insight and encouragement.
I am where I am because of you.

And this book is dedicated to You, my kind Reader.
I celebrate your choice to incarnate human.
Value your Life.
Value the contribution you are to our world.

As you explore and radiate your Light,
you contribute to the awakening of each Life you touch.

Thank You for that.

Table of Contents

Thanks for Riding Along with Me
1

Chapter 1
The Zaniness of Being Human
5
*"Here we are... colored streamers flying...
crash helmets more or less secure... hanging on for The Ride."*

Chapter 2
Your B.E.I.N.G.
Your Bio Energy Incarnate Navigation Gear
37
*"Of course this all plays out inside the nuanced
parameters of that kickin' construct of space and time."*

Chapter 3
Fluency
77
*"Meditation expands and articulates...
far beyond anything you could have first imagined."*

Chapter 4
HumanNess 101
117
"Whoa, Baby… prepare to be astonished!"

Chapter 5
3 Steps to Greater Awareness
177
"Feed that dog."

Acknowledgments
229

About the Author
231

Thanks for Riding Along with Me

Okay, so right here at the get-go, I am going to tell you something about my writing style. I like words. And I like playing with them. I don't want you to think my wonderful book editor didn't catch my stylistic tendencies. Rather, she chose to let my writing be my writing. Which I hugely appreciate.

Let's start with '…'. You will learn as you read *Holy Wow!* that this book had an incredibly long gestation period. As it finally started tumbling out, it came with '…'. A breath, a beat, a moment. If using '…' was finally how things were going to get going… who was I to resist? This '…' worked well for me. And it kept working. Naturally, I hope it works well for you, too.

Over the 4 decades as *Holy Wow!* gestated, I did, of course, write other things. When I wrote, I used "tho" for "though" and "thru" for "through"… which quite naturally led to "altho" and "thru-out." When my editor, Pam, first read my Holy Wow! manuscript, she pointed out that I was using "texting language." She expressed concern that some readers might criticize my choices and think less of my work because of such abbreviations… such casual language. As I have used these spellings my entire adult Life… I pointed out that texting just finally caught up with me. I don't mean to be vexing… this is just the way I write.

I totally understand the proper and professional… and I want you to know that Pam is both. It's me that feels odd seeing "tho" and "thru" completely spelled out in my writing. That doesn't look like me. I realize those spellings are considered by some to be text shorthand. To me… they are just the more sensible way to spell those words.

On to another thing or 2. Did you know that humans devised and used numbers centuries before letters were invented? This development of numbers, counting, and recording systems was humanity's first long-distance communication tool, having a profound effect on the ability to share knowledge, transmit information and thrive. I am intrigued by this historical significance of numbers. Giving a shout out to numbers… in my writing, I use the actual numeral to indicate numbers. (Except in the rare case when a number starts a sentence… then, I spell the word rather than using the number symbol.)

I use the word "grok" to mean "deeply understand." I also use the word "connexion" to indicate ever-so-much more connected that a mere connection. Here and there I use "yeah" as an informal "yes"… not to mean "yay." You will also find the occasional unique spelling of a word, and capitalizations that indicate certain Orientation Programs and Certifications. Now and again, in the midst of a sentence, you will come across an " = " sign. As in… "This ability to have a chuckle = a most sanity-producing maneuver as you are busy being human."

There is additional creative spelling and word usage… "intellecting" or "thinkery," for instance… which, to me, are self-explanatory. The words "equipt" or "spoilt" you may recognize as the British spelling. I've always liked them spelled that way. Words are tricky little comprehension packets. You will come across "cognent," which can be seen as a blend of "cogent" and "cognitive." I use "cognent" to describe the beings who are not in incarnation, yet. And "incarnant" to describe the beings who are.

I share this with you, Dear Reader, to say… these writing nuances are neither mistakes nor oddities. They are the creative choices that make *Holy Wow!* the experience it is. I write this to thank you for riding along with me and for easing into my stylistic ways. Now, let's have some fun!

CHAPTER 1

The Zaniness of Being Human

*"Here we are... colored streamers flying...
crash helmets more or less secure...
hanging on for The Ride."*

Well, here you are being human on Planet Earth, and there's nothing you can do about it. Ha!

Actually, here you are being human on Planet Earth and there is *everything* you can do about it. And that's the blast in the patoot. Or the blessed realization.

"What's that, you say? I've got more than one choice in the matter here?" Blessed or blasted? You mean my only choice is not just careening around in my Life... kinda crazed... chaotic... out of control? Grasping wildly for a sense of... "normal"... "security"... creativity... survival? Okay. Groovy. Another Ha!

Nearly every human on Planet Earth feels out of kilter in some way(s). Have you ever felt that you don't really belong here... in this world... in this family... in this job... in this complicated, oblong Life? That's what I mean. There it is... that nebulous gnawing. Near-continuous. Gnawing away... general anxiety... self-doubt... what-if obstacles... self-inflicted limitations. Something is just not right.

It seems our natural human tendency is to be more aware of what is wrong than what is going right. Wrong with ourselves. Wrong with our Life. Wrong with other people. Wrong with the world.

Years ago, when my children were little, I sat down on the toilet one day... Ahhh, a moment to myself. As if on cue, a litany of "what you haven't done" rained down upon me... "You haven't done this!" "You haven't done that!" "You didn't even blah, blah, blah..." After several minutes of raking myself over the coals for all I had not accomplished that day... another voice piped up... "Yes, but you did do this." "You folded the laundry." "You did make that phone call." "And you have taken care of that."

Sheesh. Thanks for noticing I actually did get something *done.* Drawing a deep breath. *Thanks for sticking up for me,* thinks I.

The Zaniness of Being Human

There it was, plain as day... my tendency to actively, consistently point out all of my shortcomings... all of my own glaring inadequacies. We're always right there to pick on ourselves with all that is *not*... not right... not enough... not this... not that... choose from this long list of "not."

Not "*enough*" has a long list all its own... not enough thin... not enough tall... not enough money... not enough opportunities... not enough love. No matter what I have in my Life, "something" is missing. It's not enough. Did I mention not enough money? Yeah, I did.

So, right here at the start, I'm going to be totally up front with you about my own personal obsession. My whole adult Life, I have been thoroughly fascinated by our human "ways"... our foibles... our fears... our self-inflicted limitations. This blaring fixation we carry with all that is "wrong." The "how" and the "why" of our personal condition. I call this "The Zaniness of Being Human."

Why *zany*, you might ask? But then, you might not ask that at all. It could be that *zany* makes as much sense to you as it does to me. Zany is a cool word. And descriptive. Zany makes me think of those mad-cap rom-com movies of the '30s and '40s... harebrained schemes... dashing about... silly misunderstandings... leading to all sorts of drama and folderol. Solutions to all those dizzy situations handily accomplished in black and white.

The dictionary definition of *zany* sizes it up... "comical or ludicrous because of incongruity or strangeness... a person given to extravagant or outlandish behavior." Ludicrous. Outlandish. Comical. While hanging out here being human on Planet Earth... it is definitely to your advantage to have a hearty sense of humor. About "things"... about Life... about yourself. Being able to chuckle at the incongruous... the comical... the outlandish. All around. And within us. This ability to have a chuckle = a most sanity-producing maneuver as you are busy being human.

You also should know that I tend to capitalize the "L" in Life. I'm not trying to be cute. I capitalize that "L" out of respect. I am awed by Life. I stand totally in awe of these bodies we walk around in. This was true even before I found out about our "mental," "emotional," and "spiritual" components. This world we live in is A Miracle.

Albert Einstein said, "There are only two ways to live your life. One is as though nothing is a miracle. The other is as though everything is a miracle." I choose the miracle. "Life" deserves a capital "L."

A large component of my awe extends to my fellow humans. I like people. I've always been interested in "who" and "how" folks are. By nature, I am a "good listener." Even as a kid, friends confided in me and asked my advice. I grew up hearing many people's stories... their woes... their

The Zaniness of Being Human

doubts... trouble with relationships... short-sighted choices. Each person so different. Each so completely who they are. Their own passions and talents... their own fears and misgivings. Mired in "this"... problemed with "that." So many truly impressive variations on the theme of living a human Life.

Fascinating.

I began meditating when I was 19. I was trained to teach meditation in my early 20s. Early in my experiences with meditation... profoundly touched as I was... I began saying, "Meditation is the greatest gift you will ever give yourself." I still say that. Only because it's true. Here in my mid-60s... I find ever more depth and dimensionality in that truth.

One of the most brilliant gifts of meditation? You... becoming aware of aspects of yourself that you had never imagined nor even considered. The reason this is so... is because you meditate in your *spiritual* body. You do not meditate in your thinkery... nor in your feeling nature.

Your ongoing experience of meditating acquaints you with features of your inner panorama your eyes have not yet opened to.

Meditation is not what you think.

Meditation is a practice. As you practice... quieting... deepening... allowing... meditation reveals itself to you.

As you practice... you discover more about yourself... this Life you are creating... this world you live in. Meditation reveals yourself to you. In a good way.

Just so you know... there wasn't any great impulse of deep spiritual seeking that took me toward meditation. It was the Beatles.

It was the late '60s. I was married to Bob. He sang and played guitar in a rock 'n' roll band. I sang, too... as I shook the tambourine and maracas... occasionally all 3 at the same time. Look out.

Bob and I actually met on a dark and stormy night. I was talking on the phone to my friend, Linda. It was so stormy that the lines kept getting crossed on the telephone. We'd hear a *brzzzt!*... and all of a sudden, another person would be on the line... wondering how in the world they ended up talking with us. It happened 4 times that night. Bob was #3.

There I was... at 15... set up with my Life's first truly defining moment. Connecting with Bob... my first boyfriend... my first husband... affected my Life in every possible way. An electrical *brzzzt!* in the phone lines... and there he was. And there we were. The Fickle Finger of Fate. Life came and got me young.

One of my favorite personal claims to fame... I attended every Beatles concert ever held in the Los Angeles area.

True story. (Do you have any idea what A Big Deal that was at the time?) The very first L.A. Beatles concert was at the Hollywood Bowl. This was the first time I was at a concert... just me and my friends. I screamed 'til I lost my voice. So cool.

John was my favorite Beatle. It didn't bother me that he was married. At 14, it wasn't like I thought *I* was going to marry him. I did, however, wear black leather, and I ironed my hair so it was long and straight. I'd read that John liked hair that way. I used cool "British" words like, "fab" and "gear." I knew all the words to "I Want To Hold Your Hand." I watched every Beatles appearance on The Ed Sullivan Show. I was stoked.

The fateful phone *brzzzt!* bringing Bob into my Life happened a few months after the Hollywood Bowl concert. All of the following L.A. Beatles concerts were held at Dodger Stadium. Bob and I were at every one of them.

I was 18 when Bob and I got married. He had just turned 19... 17 days before our wedding. Our home was adorned with Beatle posters... incense burners... and a gracious antique "secretary" which Bob's grandmother had given me. We used a lovely, drop-leaf table with Jacobean carved legs as our dining table. We purchased it from the managers of our apartment complex. They brought the table around Cape Horn when they traveled from England to the U.S. decades earlier. Lo, these many years later... I still use that table and the secretary.

Bob painted a 5'x5' psychedelic portrait of the musician, Donovan... all bright orange and yellow and neon blue. This welcomed you as you entered our front door. Of course, we owned every Beatles album... including platters pressed in England. We were *that* cool.

We began to hear that The Beatles were hanging out in India... meditating with Maharishi Mahesh Yogi. Intriguing. Maharishi originated "Transcendental Meditation" (TM)... based within the Vedic traditions of his Master, Brahmananda Saraswati. *The Beatles are doing TM! Let's go check it out!* That's how I began meditating. No great spiritual urge nor divine guidance. I wasn't searching for my path or for greater awareness. It was the Beatles. And Maharishi.

Well, and Bob. Meeting Bob at the tender age of 15... I went from being "my parents' daughter" to being Bob-and-Dana. "Hi, I'm Bob-and-Dana." We did everything Bob wanted to do... because there really wasn't anything Dana wanted to do. I went with Bob to his archery meets... sat in on his guitar lessons... was by his side as he became captivated with photography. I envied him... that he could be so impassioned with his interests. So captured. So engaged.

We were each "only" children. After we married, in our 2-bedroom apartment, we each had our own room. One bedroom was Bob's room... his darkroom and photo studio. One bedroom was mine... basically defined by artsy clutter. Our queen-size bed was in the living room. The sepia "Two Virgins" poster of John and Yoko, standing naked, front and back, was the centerpiece on the wall above our bed.

Thru-out my Life I have had what I call "previews of coming attractions." Some are teensy, others large and kind of amazing. It starts with... I am thinking about something... or my mind is wandering with its own little daydreams. I don't know that I am "previewing." I am just musing. Later... the event I was musing about... the "attraction"... shows up in my Life. I then see that all along I had been given "previews."

At Toluca Lake Elementary School... Sun Valley Junior High... and Verdugo Hills High School... I would stand in front of each of these schools I attended... looking at the houses across the street, and wonder, "What would it be like to live across the street from a school?"

As we prepared to get married, Bob and I went apartment hunting. We saw an ad in the paper offering a 2-bedroom apartment in our price range... in North Hollywood. We drove to the address and found the manager's office. This was a complex of about a dozen 4-plexes built in the early '40s. With the manager, we snaked thru the complex as she led us to the unit for rent. We climbed the back stairs and entered the kitchen. The rooms were large with big windows. Even with all the window blinds closed, it was obvious there was plenty of light. Walking around, we liked what we saw. "We'll take it." As Bob chatted details with the nice manager lady, I thought, *I wonder what the view is out the front window.* I lifted a slat in the blinds to look out. There... directly across the street... was the front of my junior high school. Well how about that!

Five years earlier, I stood right there... wondering. Now, here I was... living "across the street from a school." My school. Ok, then. A teensy "preview fulfillment"... but notable.

Spurred by The Beatles' involvement... it was Bob who wanted to check out Transcendental Meditation. Naturally, I went right along. June, 1969, found Bob and Dana at the TM Center in Westwood, near UCLA... at an introductory evening for TM. We liked what we heard. We signed right up.

The very next Saturday... we returned to the TM Center and received our mantras. For hours, we each sat alone in a room "meditating"... whatever that meant. It was very quiet... with precious few external distractions. Yes, it was kinda boring. I had absolutely no idea what I was supposed to be doing. We hung in there. As we were leaving the TM Center that Saturday, we were told to come back once a week for a series of classes to learn more about meditation. We never did that. We took our mantras and went home.

Driving home that evening... as we crested the rise on the 405 freeway with the twinkling lights of the San Fernando Valley sprawling out before us... I turned to Bob and said, "I feel like a person who has always loved ice cream, but the only flavor I knew about was vanilla. Now, all of a sudden... I've been turned on to 31 Flavors." (Little did I know...) "31 Flavors" is a popular chain of ice cream stores, also known as Baskin-Robbins. Years later, recalling my statement... I was pretty impressed that I had come up with such a creamy, spot-on metaphor right at the very beginning of my experience with meditation. From "only vanilla" to "31 Flavors"... an apt description of the tasty, dimensionalizing effect meditation brings. Life's many flavors... enhanced.

We'd been told to meditate for 20 minutes in the morning and 20 minutes in the evening. Okay. Early on, it became clear that I have a back built to meditate. From the get-go, sitting to meditate has always been comfortable for me. Bonus. Repeating my meditation mantra in my head... I had no idea what I was doing. Twice a day I sat... diligently. I liked it.

Before we got married, Bob and I were both working part-time... attending the same college... both Art majors.

When we married... Bob continued in school full time... and my part-time bank job became a full-time bank job. Ours was the common scenario... I worked to support us as he went to school.

We did cool things. The week after we received our TM mantras... we were rocking with Elton John outdoors at The Greek Theatre, near the Griffith Park Observatory. And we were totally in the groove as we watched an early stage production of the musical, *Hair*. We frequented various smoky music clubs on the Sunset Strip, where we were much more into Arthur Lee and his band, Love... than Jim Morrison and The Doors.

With about 50 other people, we experienced an incredible evening at an intimate Jimi Hendrix performance that went on for more than 4 hours. After playing for an hour and a half... Jimi told us he wasn't happy with the quality of the speakers and sent for others... which just arrived. If we didn't mind waiting as his crew changed them out... he would continue playing. Sure, Jimi... we don't mind. He played for another couple hours. It was a wonder. Jimi Hendrix was so much more than a psychedelic rock icon. What an engaging performer! A consummate musician... he was warm and congenial... funny... connected. More than I would have ever imagined. Ok, so I figured he'd be a hollowed-out stoner. Wrong. We could have been sitting in his living room as he jammed with friends. It was terrific. I was blown away.

As well as listening to The Beatles and The Rolling Stones, we attended concerts by Donovan... The Byrds... Crosby, Stills and Nash... Jefferson Airplane. We especially grooved on the bands Cream and Blind Faith. There was a sweet rhythm to our first year and a half of married Life. It worked.

And then... things changed. Within 3 months of receiving my meditation mantra... my Life turned totally inside out and completely upside down. I realized later... it was as if meditation entered my Life and said, "Ha! You thought you were going *that* way?" *Fwoop! Zoop! Voila!* Major change of course. "Now you're going *this* way!"

Bob decided he was in love with a woman he went to school with. She decided she was in love with him. Evidently, I had become the boring ol' bank teller. (Sure... I *know*. I was the one who was supporting us so he could go to school. That somehow fell out of the "let's take this into account" equation.) Over a period of several very difficult months... our marriage ended... painfully for me. It was the most emotionally excruciating thing that had happened in my sweet, short Life.

There I was... reeling... staggering thru a Life that did not feel like my own. Betrayed by my best friend. On my own at 20.

I meditated twice a day, because it was the only sane thing happening to me.

I had not once thought... *Meditation is going to save me! Meditation is going to make this better.* It did not occur to me that meditation was "spiritual"... or that it was going to "do" or "change" anything in my Life. Remember, we didn't go to those "tell you all about meditation" classes. As I continued meditating daily, I simply found that those 20 minutes... before I went to work and when I came home... were times when my inner anguish relaxed to some degree. For most of those 20 minutes... things inside me were not quite as excruciating. The "space" provided by meditating brought me a little peace. A bit of calm. Stillness. Relief.

The next year and a half found me putting my Life together. Meditating twice a day... living in my own 1-bedroom apartment in Burbank. Working as a bank teller. Going to college part-time. These were the days of the Vietnam War... anti-war demonstrations... the senseless deaths at Kent State. The ensuing national chaos led to the birth of "The Experimental College" on many college campuses. Classes offered in the Experimental College were subjects outside the usual college curriculum... taught by members of the community. Perusing the Experimental College catalog at school one day... I came across a listing entitled "The Nature of The Soul." The description for the class included words like "karma"... "reincarnation"... "meditation." Hmmm... intriguing. *Right up my alley. I'll check it out.*

Early on a Saturday morning, I drive to school and find the house on campus where the class is meeting. There are about 30 other people in the room. Sitting there... I find out this is the "Introduction" to a series of lessons... a course of instruction that is going to last for 40 weeks. *Forty weeks?! That's almost a year! Really?* As he moves thru his introductory talk, Richard, the teacher, proceeds to tell me everything that has gone on in my Life for the last year and a half. Whoa. That's cool. And only a little unnerving. I return the next Saturday for Lesson 1.

I am in my very early 20s. The class meets at 10 a.m. on Saturday morning. There is partying to be had on Friday nights. Several times, I would fall into bed at 2 or 3 a.m.... thinking, *There is no way I'm going to get up and go to that class in the morning.* Bing! 8 a.m. I'm wide awake. Might as well take a shower and go. I didn't miss a class.

Over the first several weeks, the class settles into a group of 15 people. Except for 2 women who are sisters, none of us know each other. We walk in on Saturday morning... nod to each other... maybe there's a little chit chat... mainly we just sit waiting for the class to begin.

Each week, Richard guides both an opening and a closing meditation. The meditation form is not like TM at all. *(There are different ways to meditate?!) (Who knew!?)* Each week, at the close of the first meditation, Richard hands out the week's printed lesson material. He reads the whole lesson aloud as we follow along. Then we discuss. Mostly, he discusses and we listen. The lesson content is of a captivating, esoteric nature... explaining "The 7 Rays" *(There are 7 Rays?)*... "working with Light" *(What does that mean?)*... our relationship with Spirit (*okay*)... our "human vehicle" with its mental, emotional, and physical bodies (*news to me*).

Catching my attention right away... a phrase on the very first page... "Look not to the source of this material for its authenticity, but look to the application of it in your Life." *Wow*. That resonated with me the moment I read it. This statement... this suggestion... I had not heard anything like it before. The clarity, the sincerity of it immediately grabbed me. I felt somewhere deep inside me settle into place. "Look not to the source..." Don't decide this is valid because of "the past"... because of where or who it comes from. Look to how this lives in your own Life... here... now. Those words... that approach... immediately held a deep and certain right-ness for me. I felt *encouraged*. I knew I was in the right place.

The meditation form taught in The Nature of The Soul is very different from the way I have been meditating with TM. I'm still a little stunned to find out there is more than one way to meditate. Thru TM, I learned and practiced "mantric" meditation. *Mantra* is a word... a sound or phrase... repeated again and again. Focusing on the mantra... mentally repeating it... is a tool, a way to focus concentration and clear the mind of general anxiety and chatter.

As Richard begins a Nature of The Soul meditation, I am guided to give my attention to consciously relaxing my physical body. *What tension in my shoulders and upper back? Oh my gosh...* that *tension! Could my jaw muscles possibly be any more clenched? Whoa. They're really on to something here with this conscious relaxation.*

Next step... bring my emotional self to a place of balance... calm... like the still surface of a clear mountain pool. Of course, that doesn't happen immediately. Or for a long while. But, hey... it's good to practice aiming in that direction. Next, I am to quiet my thoughts... *yeah, right. Good luck with that ol' speeding freight train of constant, clamoring chatter.* After doing the best I can to quiet my thoughts... I am to lift my conscious awareness... moving upward and inward... aligning with my spiritual body. Indeed.

This is a very different way to meditate than repeating a mantra.

Richard uses the word "quiescence." Such a gorgeous word. I don't know what it means. But I like it. It makes me think of "quiet essence."

Each Nature of The Soul lesson closes with a phrase that is to be our meditation "seed thought" for the coming week. We meditate on this seed thought as we lift our awareness. We are encouraged to meditate on our own during the week... focusing on this seed thought. Meditating daily is encouraged.

I am enthralled by what I am learning.

I begin to notice that... consistently... Richard's remarks on Saturday morning elaborate on ideas or concepts I pondered or randomly thought about between classes. At the 5th class meeting, in response to one of his comments, I blurt out, "That is exactly what I've been thinking about this week!" Several other students chime in, "Me too!" We all look around at each other. Richard is very smooth. He doesn't say anything one way or the other as he proceeds with the lesson. For the first time, after class, we all go out to brunch together. We talk about the uncanny "what's going on?" in this class. Brunch after class becomes a fixture of our learning experience. Many a cheese omelet is consumed.

The Zaniness of Being Human

I am completely hooked on this esoteric training. It fascinates me like *nothing* has in my Life so far.

A flash of realization... *Oh, my gosh! I am as consumed by this experience as Bob is by his interests.* That's cool. I savor this feeling of being so engaged and *interested* in something.

I am intrigued by the information about our 3 Bodies... our physical... emotional... and mental selves. I'd never thought about it this way before. It makes so much sense. It seems like such a good idea to know this!

Included is the fact that we are *not* these bodies. We are not our physical body. We're not our feelings or emotions. We are not our thoughts. We think... we feel... we move... but that is not who we *are*. As a kid, I used to think about... *What is it that* leaves *when a person dies?* I mean, the physical body is still here... but something has obviously "left the building." What is that? I learn thru this teaching that our thoughts... our emotional reactions... our activity... our choices in Life... are animated, guided by our Soul Conscious Awareness.

The Soul is our Animating Life Force. That's what "leaves" when a person dies.

This lesson material presents so much clarifying information about our inner workings. I never thought about any of this before. Yet, once pointed out... this is all immediately so clear and totally useful to realize. The meditations... the concepts discussed... the "way" of it all... stimulates my thinking... my awareness... in a manner I had no idea was even available to consider.

I am lifted out of the dust cloud of reclaiming my Life after Bob's betrayal and our divorce. I begin to feel like "myself" in a way I didn't even know was possible.

I change jobs... moving on from the bank. A referral thru customers I meet at the bank leads me to become The Portfolio Room Queen at the newly opened California Institute of The Arts in Valencia, California. Cal Arts is made up of a number of performing arts schools. Students submit portfolios to be considered for admission. My job is to receive the Art and Film portfolios and present them to the admissions committees of the related schools. This is a job I am well-suited for.

This is definitely a job with its own cool perks. Ravi Shankar... already famous for playing with George Harrison... is on the Board of Directors. He regularly gives free concerts for students and staff. Beyond cool. And *much* to my delight...the Music School includes a traditional Javanese Gamelan (GAM uh lawn) orchestra. They, too, give regular performances. A place in me absolutely sparkles as I listen to this exotic ear candy.

I learn from one of the Gamelan musicians... when young children display an interest in the Gamelan instruments...

they are encouraged to play with the bells... the drums... the xylophones. If a child shows no interest in the instruments... rather than being forced to learn Gamelan... they are encouraged to explore other things. Note to self: When you become a parent, Dana... utilize this approach.

Art, film, sculpture, music... Cal Arts is my kind of place. I move into a house near the campus with 3 other Nature of The Soul students whom I've gotten jobs at Cal Arts. I work... I meditate... I study The Nature of The Soul. Life develops a pleasing rhythm... a welcomed, purposeful *hum*.

I have a clear memory of walking around Cal Arts aware of a great, raw "hole" inside me... the painful absence of my relationship with Bob and all the space it had taken up in my Life. We'd been a couple for more than 5 years... a quarter of my Life, at that point. I don't know if it's because of the material I am studying... or just my general nature... but I realize that filling this hole "with a man"... another absorbing, distracting relationship... is not what I need to do. Heaven knows, Cal Arts presents a lot of attractive, artistic men... students... faculty... staff. It's certainly tempting. Part of me thinks... *You know, Dana, finding another man would be easiest.* Yet, another place in me deeply knows... insists... I need to fill this hole with myself. *(Whatever that means.)*

In all of the hurting and anguish churning inside me... even tho I felt deeply wounded... I did not blame Bob for the choice he had made. And I couldn't blame "her" either, because he was an attractive, talented guy. My "way" was to ride hard on myself. Perhaps this "way" has come up for you in your Life. The litany sounding something like this... "What's the matter with me?" "Why doesn't he want to be with me?" And, of course, the perennial favorite... "What's *she* got that *I* don't have?"

As my Life moved on... this was deep, damaged misery I just had to slog thru.

Even tho I didn't know what I was doing as I meditated... and I didn't anticipate meditation "fixing me"... I can tell you with certainty... meditation played a hugely significant role as I pulled myself together and got on with my Life.

I have always found great value in this piece of wisdom from Nelson Mandela: "As I walked out the door toward the gate that would lead to my freedom, I knew if I didn't leave my bitterness and hatred behind, I'd still be in prison." As I recall his words, I remember how... a year or 2 after our divorce... I realized that I could have been so bitter... so resentful... mired in sorrow. And I could have held on to it. Clasped it around my heart. I could have worn my misery like a badge. My agonizing cloak of pain. Wounding myself again and again. I could have let the bitterness have me... define me. But I didn't.

I'm not going to say this was something I gave huge, conscious thought to. Thankfully, it didn't occur to me to wallow in my misery and stay stuck there. In ways that made sense to me at the time... I just kept putting one foot in front of the other.

Sometimes it was a slog. *Poor me*. Sometimes it was twinkle toes. *Yay, Life!* Mostly, it was just getting on with it. *Next.*

I'm not going to tell you I felt "guided"... that would be a stretch. But I did keep moving. And fascinating events... connexions... possibilities... did show up. Sometimes I would wallow. But I did not allow the pain and betrayal to mold me. I am beyond grateful that it did not occur to me to let bitterness shape... define... my relationship with my Life. Thanks, Goodness.

As Life went on... I came to refer to the traumatizing experience of Bob falling in love with another woman... as "the scar that turned into a beauty mark."

All of this trauma and despair occurred in my Life during the year and a half between when I first received my TM mantra and when I walked into the Introductory class of The Nature of The Soul. Walking into that class... I was no longer who I thought I was. My underpinnings had been wrenched out from under me. Between struggling, laughing, and moving on... I was ripe for transformation.

More than a year after I begin studying The Nature of The Soul, Richard offers a "Teacher Training" class. I sign right up. Most of the other students in my class do, too. These Teacher Training classes meet weekly for many months. Arriving in Orange County for the first evening of Teacher Training, we meet other Nature of The Soul students from Richard's classes in Santa Monica, Fullerton, and Culver City. The lesson material in Teacher Training is even more engrossing and "out there" than our original training. *Whoa. Groovy.*

This was the very early '70s. We students feel we are involved in something beyond extraordinary. We are learning about being human and being spirit in a way everyone would find helpful to understand. But few ever do.

Saturday, late afternoon, we all pile into 3 or 4 cars and drive south for more than an hour, to a lovely home in La Mirada. The Nabisco cookie factory is nearby. I will always associate the heavenly smell of baking cookies with deep, esoteric information. Not bad, as associations go.

We would arrive... meet... greet... meditate... have our perceptions uplifted... our minds blown. Late in the evening, on our way back home... our heads spinning... our consciousness deliciously elevated... we'd stop in a

The Zaniness of Being Human

24-hour hotel dining room to debrief. Many more cheese omelets consumed.

Thru The Nature of The Soul Teacher Training, I learn to guide others in meditation. Of all the 20-plus students in our Teacher Training class... I am the first one offered a Nature of The Soul class to teach. An honor, for sure. And completely terrifying. *Me?!* Richard assures me, "I'll be right there with you. We'll co-teach the class."

Our co-taught class begins. The lesson for each class is several pages of printed material. In preparation every week, I industriously study these pages. My role in the class is to direct some of the conversation based on the lesson material. Richard leads most of the discussion and guides the beginning and closing meditations, which are the mainstay of the class. I am grateful for a gentle, supported entry into teaching this deep, insightful material.

We are teaching this class in the same house on campus where my first Nature of The Soul class met. Week 6... 10 a.m.... the students and I arrive for class. We howdy each other and visit. It's 10 minutes after 10:00. We're all waiting... patiently... for Richard to arrive. More minutes go by. Richard is late. It's 10:30. Richard is later. Okay. It's becoming pretty clear that Richard is a no-show. *Has something happened to him? Should I be worried? Or just really freaked out?*

It doesn't take me long to figure out Richard's "training plan" for new teachers. It's yours now, Honey. Sink or swim. He never comes to this new class again.

Oh look... I'm teaching The Nature of The Soul completely on my own. *(Say what?!)*

This "turn of events" means it is mine to guide the 2 meditations each Saturday. Wowza! I guided a few meditations as an exercise during the Teacher Training classes. Even tho, at this point, I have been meditating for more than 3 years... it's a whole different thing to guide a meditation for myself than it is to guide a group of other people in meditation. Basically, I have *no* idea what I am doing. Here are all these students in class... looking at me like I know something. Waiting for me... The Teacher... to guide them. Holy cows!

Stretching far beyond my known universe. Many deep breaths. Waves of panic. Stretching way out there some more. *Really...* out... there. "Let us prepare to meditate..."

Ok, so what do you know? Learning by doing = the best way to learn. Sinking... can indeed lead to swimming.

I see that now. The "wisdom" of Richard's way. Back then... in that moment... opening my mouth to guide an uplifting experience for these students... holding (finding) the higher alignment... was beyond dire. It was completely terrifying. I felt like such an impostor. I was more than aware of all I did not know. *Me?! Who am I to be guiding these people in meditation?*

Yet, the feedback I got from these people... their comments during and after class... told me they were having an insightful, lifting experience. *Really?! Really? Okay, then. Onward.*

I'm not going to tell you I was thrilled with Richard's "just not showing up" teacher training style. Okay, I was pretty put out. And totally freaked... even as I managed to maintain a calm, mostly smooth external demeanor. Yet, what do you know? There really isn't a better way to learn to guide meditation... than to guide meditation.

Richard obviously knew what was what. So... by "just doing it"... I became a meditation teacher.

Whereas, I knew I didn't want to be defined by the bitterness of my divorce... I can easily say that my adult Life has been completely "defined" by my Nature of The Soul training. I remember thinking even before the Teacher Training classes... *If I am receiving this training... this caliber of information... at such a young age... what* is *the rest of this incarnation going to be like?!"* Experiencing this insightful teaching in my early 20s "set my feet firmly upon my Path." The blessing burns bright.

I taught Nature of The Soul classes for 15 years. Always in groups that included both women and men... as the groups were configured in The Nature of The Soul and Teacher Training classes where I was trained. I was teaching a class in the mid-'80s when a random occurrence completely changed the trajectory of my meditation-teaching future.

This fateful Nature of The Soul class was a group of 9 women and 6 men. Remember, this training is a process that is almost a year long. We were past Lesson 20 when, one night… all for totally different reasons… the 6 men were absent from class. Each called me during the week to say they would not be attending. As far as I knew, all of the women students would be at the class. I didn't think a thing of it as I prepared to teach that week's lesson.

Little did I know what was about to unfold.

We women all arrived and warmly greeted each other. As we settled in and began the opening meditation… something extraordinary happened. Everything felt different. The only way I have ever been able to describe it… "it felt like rich, brown velvet." All of us women meditating together was… unexpectedly… a completely "other" experience. It had a totally different *feel* to it. We all felt it. And were amazed.

It had never occurred to me that meditating with only women would be any different from what my friend, Rev. Ed Townley, would call an "all skate." But different it was.

The next week, the men all returned and we continued thru to the end of the lesson series.

The Zaniness of Being Human

But from the end of that class onward, I have worked almost exclusively with women. Not teaching The Nature of The Soul... but offering... thru the '80s and into the '90s... what I called Women's Spiritual Support Groups. Tho the focus of the groups is very similar... over the decades, the "title" of my women's groups has evolved to Women's Spirit Circles.

Of course, these Women's Circles include guided meditation... and I come prepared with a topic to share and deepen into. I sometimes include printed "party favors"... cards I make with lovely art and different pithy phrases and spiritual friendly reminders. One of my favorites is:

> I Am Loved.
> I Am Loving.
> I Am Love.

And I am quite clear... I don't have to always be the one talking. I am not the only woman present with something insightful to share. The very best part of these Women's Circles is passing the talking stick. Each woman in the Circle has an opportunity to share what's up with her. Sometimes I'll ask a particular question... or say "tell us about..." But usually, the talking stick is an open invitation for a woman to share whatever she'd like.

Over these decades of offering Women's Circles, I have found it fascinating... and rewarding... to watch the first night a new group meets. It is clear that some of the women who are there for the first time are trepidatious. Some women have even said to me... "Everybody here has it so much more together than I do." By the end of that first evening... having heard parts of each woman's story in the course of the group discussion and as the talking stick passes hand to hand... these new women are completely at ease. Their "takeaway" being: "Everyone here is just like me." It is a wonder to behold. How beautifully we all fit together.

Over all these years, I have also offered private spiritual counseling with personal guided meditation. All told... I have been teaching others to meditate for more than 45 years. Lucky me.

It could be said, all these years I have been obsessed with meditation. But, that's really just shorthand. To acknowledge more clearly what captivates me... we come back to "The Zaniness of Being Human."

As I mentioned... the definition of *zany* says, "being comical or ludicrous because of incongruity or strangeness, a person given to extravagant or outlandish, eccentric behavior." Over the years, I noticed that we are each pretty "eccentric"... a little "outlandish"... definitely unique. Truly... it is as if we each live on our own private planet. We travel our own terrain. We come with our distinct set of inner and outer coordinates... along with our own personal scenery. We are individually wired to determine what *this* means... and how *that* is going to affect me. And then there's that distinctive cast of fascinating characters we each get to encounter and interact with.

Let's face it... we humans are pretty comical folk. Twisted. Insecure. Divine.

Heaven knows there is Great Advantage in being blessed with an agreeable sense of humor. Let's have a good chuckle, shall we? This travels hand-in-hand with developing our ability to choose to be amused rather than annoyed. Watch out for that "I'm so annoyed." It's a slippery slope... generally taking you somewhere you don't really want to go.

My obsession? That ever-fascinating interplay... of "All that is being human"... cruising thru the intersection of "All that Life has to offer." Watch those changing traffic lights. Green means GO. Red means STOP. Yellow means "Watch out for everything in between." There are choices to be made. You can either be in the road... or on the sidewalk. Running. Strolling. Bicycling. Skateboarding. Revving your engine. Traveling with traffic or against traffic. Choose wisely, Grasshopper. It can be a bumpy ride. There's always "cruise control." Remember to use those turn signals.

There is that which lifts us up and that which tears us down. Or, more accurately... that which gives us the opportunity to lift ourselves up... and that which gives us the opportunity to tear ourselves down.

Turns out Life offers plenty of both... lifting up... tearing down... lifting up some more.

It also turns out... there is plenty of what we can and cannot do about it. Plenty of what we do about it. Plenty of what we do *not* do.

This is where my story begins. Where each of us stands. At that oh-so-human intersection of chaos and skill... clarity and confusion... waking up and shutting down... laughter and tears... love and fear.

Here we are... colored streamers flying... crash helmets more-or-less secure... hanging on for The Ride.

Strike up the band!

Let the fireworks begin.

We're on our way!

CHAPTER 2

Your B.E.I.N.G.
Your Bio Energy Incarnate Navigation Gear

"Of course this all plays out inside the nuanced parameters of that kickin' construct of space and time."

"Testing. Testing."
"May I have your attention? Hello? Is this telepathy amplifier operating?"
"Testing. Hello? Ah... there. Now I can hear myself think."
"Cognitive units, please settle in. Prepare to receive transmission. Your Orientation Moment begins now." Greetings, cognent beings. Welcome to The Interpretorium.

As your Orientation Activities Director, I am delighted to welcome you to Incarnation Prep... your first step into incarnating human. Here, you will begin to arrange your cognitive essence and prepare to individuate. As you get to know your Incarnant Paraphernalia... you will cross the threshold into that Grand and Glorious MultiPlex Adventure... Incarnating Human on Planet Earth (I. H.O.P.E.).

Planet Earth is a prime destination resort. It is one of our most popular incarnant locales. It's no surprise that this exquisite blue-green orb is a top-pick venue. The Physical Plant Department really has outdone itself. The prime terrain and sweeping scenery on Planet Earth cannot be beat... precipitous mountains... stunning evergreens... vibrant sunsets... flora *and* fauna. And covering nearly three-quarters of the globe... a liquid blue aqua firma abundant with Life.

Your Bio Energy Incarnate Navigation Gear (your B.E.I.N.G.) is a remarkable piece of equipment. Not only is Planet Earth endowed with the Ultimate Fragrance Upgrade... this human instrument you will inhabit is fully equipt with the olfactory receptors to enjoy it. Yes, there will be gardenias.

Responding to the many requests... I am happy to tell you that both pineapple and avocado are being served on Planet Earth right now. And, you... incarnating with your bright and bold taste receptors… ready to savor it all.

Another perk... The Kahunas of Music graced Planet Earth long ago. The air itself is embroidered with birdsong. And you... with your Enhanced Audio Receptor System will be able to hear it all! You'll be well-equipt to take in the melody of Life... absorbing... cherishing. Sweet overtones and deep undertones. Is this totally splendid, or what?

The Earthtone setting and scenery are, of course, superb. But let's face it, folks... the genuine attraction... the real reason you're here to prep and head on into incarnation... is for the thrill of the Human Vehicle you get to inhabit... equipt as it is with all of its P.E.P.: your Prime Experience Portals.

You can't fool me. I know what *you* are looking for. That Human Vehicle on Planet Earth comes complete with a fine assortment of delectable nuances... multi-grade pleasure sensors... and, yes, it's true... your very own engaging set of random foibles. You will find your tri-body incarnant gear to be a device resplendent with both hardware and software. You'll have a physical instrument... an emotional nature... and a somewhat developed mental apparatus. Touching, tasting... responding to Life with all 3 of these indicators at the same time. Thinking... feeling... doing... ahhh... the vast possibilities of engaging your realm. Myriad idiosyncrasies. Endless amusement.

So many cognitive units clamor to incarnate in this tri-body vehicle on that luscious blue-green orb... we had to instigate a system of lotteries. We want to guarantee fair and equal access to this Supreme Opportunity to individuate and *experience...* right in the midst of such an engaging and popular venue.

And here you all are... lucky lottery winners! Congratulations!

Here at The Interpretorium... you'll receive the standard refresher course in Incarnate Embodiment... as well as updates on current planetary customs... circumstances and conditions. Of course, this all plays out inside the nuanced parameters of that kickin' construct of space and time. I know you are looking forward to this upcoming opportunity to engage in the general zaniness of being human and this whirl of unprecedented commotion. As you know... Planetary Incarnation Earth (P.I.E.) also offers you an extensive variety of consequences, situations, and upliftments... all delectable slices of *that* juicy P.I.E. You are in for such a treat!

As enchanting as this all sounds... most of you are aware of the true and baffling fascination this captivating venue holds. Right in the middle of the elaborate assortment of Earthtone possibilities... each incarnate human lives in their own unique world.

Inhabiting the very core of your B.E.I.N.G. is a distilled drop of your cognitive essence. This drop... this spark...

enlivens your incarnate process... starting the ball a'rollin' toward personhood. As a "person," you will reside within your own Absolutely Created Existence (A.C.E.). Your A.C.E. is structured on a framework of karmic assertions... particular talents... general aptitudes... and overall attitudes. Your human experience is enlivened by your own unique cast of characters... opportunities... self-inflicted limitations... and ego-driven vexations.

Motivating along in your incarnate vehicle... in every split-second in time... you will personally interpret... catalogue... and categorize... every incoming nuance and aspect of your human existence. Your *interpretations* weave the fabric of your Life. Your interpretations render the texture of your beliefs. Is my Life *good* or *bad*? Is it *as it should be* or *totally screwed up*? Your inner story... the narrative of how you explain it all to yourself... will be your A.C.E. in The Whole.

This is, of course, wisely articulated by Geraldine, Bard of Flip: "What you see is what you get!"

Are you wondering why this incarnate preparation arena is called The Interpretorium? Well, here's the reason: Your A.C.E. in The Whole... your upcoming human interpreting mechanism... plays a totally significant role in the quality of your human Life on Earth. As you interpret each and every thing... so do you believe. About your self... your talents and your limitations. About your Life... your opportunities and your struggles. About other people... they're *like* me... they're *not like* me. Interpretation. You get to call it... *this* is what's happening to me.

On Planet Earth, the weather is just the weather. Whether the weather is *good* or *bad* is based on your interpretation of the weather. Human Life is just Human Life. Whether yours is a *good* Human Life or a *bad* Human Life is based solely upon your interpretation of what is.

Here at The Interpretorium, we give our utmost to prepare you for Your Best Human Life Possible. As a matter of fact... coming as we are from this current realm of pure cognition... The Interpretorium is synonymous with *Let's Go Be Living Human on Planet Earth*. On Earth... truer than true... what you see... how you call it... *is* what you get. How you believe it is... is *it*. Each incarnate human resides within their own interpretations of who they are and what's going on.

What else could this place be called *but* The Interpretorium?

Existing as you will within Earth's vast and wide spectrum... between delight, despair, and delirium... you get to call it. The "what it is" and the "who I am" are all sculpted upon your inner rendition... your own version of your Life's "what's what" aspects.

While you are human... you'll spend a lot of time wanting to think any experience of difficulty or despair is about someone else. Whatever "it" is... it's "their fault." For years, decades, incarnations... you'll be tempted to play the victim... blaming obstacles, doubts, and difficulties on other people. At some point... your moment of clarity will arrive. You look around at how things are. Sizing up your perspective on it all. Blaming others for this and that. How's that working for you?

A time does come when, upon evaluation... you'll realize that this approach of blaming and finding fault with "others" simply does not serve your general growth and development. You will find that, in truth... blaming others does you no good what so ever.

Actually, this is one of the trick features of the human experience. Your human instrument... and the Life it creates for itself on Planet Earth... are completely at the mercy of your "what I tell myself is happening." Oh, that. And your habits... physical, mental, and emotional. These 2 inner mechanisms... your interpretations and your habits... will shape and color your entire interactive engagement on Planet Earth.

Your "version" of what you tell yourself is happening to you becomes exactly what *is* happening to you. I know, residing here... not yet in human form... you're like all, "yeah, sure, fine." But truth is… this clarity you experience here will not be all that clear when you are personhooding. Many aspects of Life and being that are so forthright here… you'll find are "not so much" there on Planet Earth.

For now… best we simply move on, as we have a large assemblage of content to cover. Ha! You could call it an "assemblarge." Ha ha. Okay. Right, then.

This may be jumping ahead a bit… but before we get down to the actual nitty-gritty of your Review and Update Material… I'm thinking it would be fun to go ahead and engage your "Simulant Tri-Body Human" Bio Energy Suit.

This B.E. Suit simulates the basic features of the actual Bio Energy Incarnate Navigation Gear you will inhabit on Planet Earth. Here at Team Interpretorium, we've devised this simulant model to give you an opportunity to familiarize yourself with some of the attributes of the equipment your spark of cognition will be cruising around in.

You'll find this 3 Body Earthtone Action Model… your 3 B.E.A.M.… quite outstanding… downright captivating… with all of its physical, emotional, and mental bio-gear. Thinking. Aspiring. Feeling. Touching. Emoting. Contorting. Leaping. Dancing. A dizzying array of sensation and activity!

Here today, you will each deploy in the standard Healthy Young Adult Model, which has been programmed to the physical equivalent of a human in their early 30s.

You'll find your Tri-Body Simulator easy to engage. Let's have at it.

Go ahead. Shaking it out some will make it easier to slip into your simulant. As you don your B.E. Suit... I will be adjusting mine, as well. Thus, we will begin together our descent into the delight and delusion of density. Prime yourself for an unusual, yet not unpleasant, series of sensations.

You will know you are reaching full installation of your B.E. Suit when you begin to notice the hum, thump, and swish of the physical upkeep system. At first, this clamor will seem rather deafening... with all the pulsing, ticking, and plumbing sounds of the physical plant functions. That throbbing boom, boom, boom is your "heart-beat"... the cadence of your highly essential pump apparatus. Be glad for this throbbing. Your physical unit will not make it far without it.

You will be amazed how quickly this consuming roar fades into the background. As you become increasingly engaged with your human sensory input... your interpretive perceptions... and your various activities of daily living... this bio-maintenance cacophony will fade to near silent. Truly. It will.

Now that your tri-body suits are in place... instead of engaging you telepathically, as I have been... I will commence communicating via my "voice." This will be accomplished as I transmit vocal pulsations suited to the density of the physical plane. You will receive these pulsations thru your instrument's Enhanced Audio Receptor System. You will find that your E.A.R.S. come in a dandy matching pair... situated for maximum input efficiency on either side of your human "head."

Pardon me, as I engage my vocal apparatus. Just a moment... ahem. I'll just clear my pipes. Gack. Gaw-hemk. Okay. Ahem... there. Now I've got the hang of it. Oh... ha! I'd forgotten. "Vocalizing" generates a pleasurable little hummy vibration... a tickle in the voice's box. Sweet. Okay. Here we go.

As I "speak"... I emit shaped sound vibrations which the E.A.R.S. of your B.E. Suit will process as incoming tonal modulation. Can you hear me now?

The sound reverberation of my voice vibrates the hearing mechanisms built inside your E.A.R.S. This sends a tone pulse to your "brain" for scanning and explication. Your brain is your human vehicle's multi-frequency interpretive apparatus. My vocal tones are shaped into comprehension units called *words*. What comes next is a rather cumbersome process... please attend carefully to how this works. Referencing reams of incarnant data... your brain... roving thru your internal compilation of attitudes and experience filters... translates the audio grab of my words into concepts and information. This activity generates your perception of what is being conveyed.

Physically, my words vibrate your auditory mechanism. Transitioning beyond the physical... these verbal comprehension units... travel thru various incarnant and karmic interpretive filters. Your brain receptors are stimulated to then understand what is being conveyed. Accustomed as you are here... to the simple and direct thought transference of telepathy... this is, indeed, a laborious approach to communication processing. Kinda clunky. This is one of many accommodations that must be made to utilize the receptor units of your Earthtone instrument.

Not only is this laborious... it is also a very *tricky* system. Let me just say, it is best to not assume this transmission of spoken and then heard communication is always clarity-inducing. You will... at times... experience unexpected and inexplicable communication outcomes. These inexplicable outcomes can lead to actual breakdowns in the transmission of information. What you are "saying" is not always "heard" by the other person as what you intended. As you are using "words," merely sharing an observation might be heard by the other person as an insult. Why is that, you might ask? You're right... times like those are both clumsy *and* frustrating. Yes... this *does* lead to unintentional gaffes... misunderstandings... conflict, even. But here's the deal...

up until Intuition and Instantaneous Knowing become more developed in the human instrument... this clunky communication modality is what we've got to work with.

Tho, I am going to tell you this... when communication between humans does work... 'tis a lovely thing. Despite an array of obstacle illusions... humans do manage to connect. Beauteous. Harmony prevails. Well worth the effort.

While incarnate, you will generally find your entire Enhanced Auditory Receptor System to be a true pleasure. The Nature of Sound has moved far beyond the Sound of Nature... wondrous tho that is. As I mentioned... eons ago, The Kahunas of Music bequeathed their sonorous touch upon Planet Earth. Such sweet, melodious favors. Happily, the human vehicle is imbued with the blessed capacity to both hear and *create...* melody... tone... harmony... composition. Chants! Tunes! Arias! Such variety!

Over the eons... humans have ingeniously applied this melodic gift to devise a vast number of different musical "instruments." These are played upon in various ways. Some of these instruments have tuned strings, which are plucked or strummed... some are different shaped reeds and tubes which are blown thru. Others get banged on. Very clever human devising. Just watch them humans embrace and augment their graced ability to both hear and make music!

Speaking of blowing thru musical reeds and tubes... the next experience to have in your B.E. Suit will be the stimulating of your essential respiratory capabilities. For the human instrument on Planet Earth... it is crucial to successfully engage your breathing components. An Actual Incarnate Requirement (A.I.R.)... breath is *the* basic life-sustaining implement.

Of the Life-maintaining components that keep your physical apparatus functioning... you can survive without fuel nourishment for many days... without liquid for a few days... but without breath... mere minutes. Successfully manipulating your A.I.R. modality is vital to continue playing The Game.

As you engage your respiration unit... you will find we have replicated the oxygen-rich environment of Planet Earth. This will give you a truly authentic experience as you exercise your respiratory capabilities. You will notice... on your "face"... there are 3 conveniently located air-intake ports. The larger orifice is your *mouth*. The 2 smaller portholes are called *nostrils*. These 3 ports operate interchangeably as air-handling devices.

Experiment with the procedure of breath... inhale... draw air in slowly, deeply. Feel your air sacks... the lung components in your chest... filling with air. The first few times you release breath... or exhale... there will be a snort...

kind of a pop. To avoid that little explosive puff as the air leaves... practice allowing the air to release slowly. Inhale... filling your lungs... slowly, deeply. Exhale... release slowly... completely. After a few practice cycles... you will develop a natural rhythm. Breathing will come quite effortlessly. Inhale... Exhale. Inhale... Exhale. Within moments, this will just happen... with neither thought nor effort. Ultimately, you will give no attention to the process at all. Unless, of course, something obstructs your breathing. That, you will notice right away.

Let me state this very clearly... the thumping of your pumping heart... and the continuous in and out of The Sweet Breath of Life... are what physically fasten you to your very existence on Planet Earth. Should either or both of these 2 essential components fail or not function smoothly... you're toast. In this case... "toast" is a colloquial term that has nothing to do with bread or jam. Ha ha. In this current context... "toast" means you're done for. Kaput. You've taken your seat on the right-on-out-of-incarnation express.

A smooth, assured dexterity within this most essential respiratory activity will develop as you practice managing breath thru both your nostril intake ports and thru your mouth. As I've said... after a few practice cycles, a natural cadence develops and the process becomes quite effortless.

You will move thru your entire incarnation gently riding on the rhythm of your own breath.

Familiarizing yourself with breath modulation is essential to utilizing your voice... speaking... singing... laughing... shouting. It is breath streaming thru your voice's box that creates vocal sounds and invigorates comprehension units. No breath... no talk.

And here is a superb additional benefit to breath... some call it breath "work." As you cruise around in your humanness... it will be to your great advantage to learn and practice The Fine Art of Meditation. This will give you opportunities to develop a conscious relationship with the Spark Of Ultimate Life Within that animates your thoughts, feelings, and actions. Your S.O.U.L. Within. As you are incarnate... your mental, emotional, and physical busy-ness will keep you *so* distracted. It will be a while before you even glimpse the fact that the busy-ness is not the whole go. Not even close. The busy-ness is only the "show." The "glitz." Continuous activity. Distracto Major. Keeping you far from the Essence of All Things. Here is where awareness of your breath will prove most beneficial.

Mindful breath is the basic primer of human meditation. Give your attention to your breath... inhale deeply, slowly. Exhale... releasing completely. Being mindful within your breath will gift you with experiences of calm...

clarity... insight. As you navigate the ever-engrossing arena of human Life... mindful breath will help you release from the ridiculous chatter of overthink... remind you of your possibilities... and generally clear the air inside your head... your heart... your gut... your being.

So simple. That's the beauty of it. Mindful breath is a tool you always have with you.

In human incarnation... The Blessing of Breath extends its influence far beyond the physical.

As you incorporate on Planet Earth... your actual Bio Energy Incarnate Navigation Gear comes equipt with the Classic 5 Senses Package. This Classic Package has been replicated for you here in your B.E. simulator. Your 3 respiratory intake ports do quite a lot more than just suck air. The 2 little holes... your nostril ports... also house your olfactory component... your sense of smell. These small portholes allow you the ability to detect odor and fragrance. Ahhh… food finders. Plus, your odor-detecting capability is especially helpful in identifying the stink of spoilt fuel... which, if ingested... could derail your delicate physical functions. Give it a sniff. Safe to say... if it smells bad... it is bad. Don't eat it.

There are a few exceptions to this foul-smelling rule... gorgonzola cheese... chopped red onions... extra sharp cheddar. These each reek like body odor... stinky feet. But most of you will actually find them quite delicious to ingest.

Identifying the funky and the fetid is not the only way your sniffery is useful. Your B.E.I.N.G. will be fitted with extensive olfaction action. The evolutionary processes of The Plant Kingdom, in particular, have done wonders with Earth's Ultimate Fragrance Upgrade. Your high-functioning olfactory equipment allows you complete appreciation of these many fine aromas and fragrances.

For your edification, we are now pumping into our atmosphere here a few high-grade Earthtone fragrances. Here is a human-created food item called bread... as it is baking. Ahhhh. Can you believe it?! We'll give you a full minute to relish that one. Now, a splendid contribution from the Plant Kingdom... deeply draw in the fragrance of lilacs in full bloom. Truly Divine. Here we have a 3rd sample aroma... another food item... onions and bell pepper simmering in butter. Mmmmm. Doesn't the top of your head just lift off in delight? That 3rd delicious aroma gives us a smooth segue as we begin to explore the larger of your 3 intake ports... your mouth.

Whereas utilization of your smaller, twin nostril ports is limited to breath activity and aroma detection... you will find the larger orifice... your mouth... has evolved into a delightfully complex multi-use portal. One standard mouth function is fuel consumption. This is crucial in sustaining physical body existence. Thru your mouth... you intake fuel and nutritive elements for mastication and insertion into the human digestive system. These nutritive elements are known as "food" and "fluids" or "liquid refreshment."

Turn your attention to your oral cavity. Do you detect a liquid secretion inside? This is saliva. Your saliva has currently been stimulated by the aroma of the sautéed onions and bell pepper. This saliva swimming in your mouth serves as an aid in food digestion. Practice engaging your neuromuscular reflex action of swallowing. Allow the saliva to move to the back of your mouth. As you swallow... it slides into your throat. Down the hatch it goes.

Just a helpful "social graces" note here... at times, excess saliva can dribble out of the corner of your mouth. This is called *drooling*. In most circles... the discharge of drool is considered less than attractive... possibly leading to taunting comments and other reactions of disgust. Here's a helpful suggestion... keep your drool in.

Continuing to investigate the inside of your oral cavity... have you run into that flaccid, flappy lump of flesh resting on the floor of your mouth? This is your *tongue*. Slack and blobby as it may be... the tongue itself has an impressive array of multi-purpose functions. It tastes... which we will get to in a few minutes. The tongue squirts digestive fluid... the previously-mentioned saliva... and helps move fuel particles around inside your mouth to aid in mastication.

Right now, lift your tongue up and move it around inside your mouth. You will come in contact with hard, smooth widgets in a neat semi-circle row at the top of your mouth and another matching row at the bottom. These are your *teeth*... essential for chewing and mastication. Your teeth crack and grind food matter into small bits... easy to swallow and shove down your throat for digestive processing.

Now move your tongue out beyond your teeth to the opening at the very front of your mouth. As you move your tongue around this threshold... you find there is an edge to your oral cavity... a ribbon of flesh accentuating the rim of your mouth... top and bottom. These "ribbons" are your lips. Lips are wondrous things. You have probably observed... as I've engaged my simulant's vocal capabilities and am speaking... my lips move as I shape words. Your lips will allow you to express a wide range of emotional pleasures and/or disgusts... smile... frown... kiss. You can even stick your tongue out thru your lips, if you are so inspired.

Respiration... fuel intake... mastication... these are not the only utilities your mouth, tongue, lips, and teeth provide. As you begin to exercise your own vocal capacities... you will find that the movements of your lips and mouth... your flabby lump of a tongue... and your hard teeth widgets... synch together. They will be instrumental in shaping your vocal tones into word units, which your fellow humans will understand. Your voice propelled by your breath + the synchronized movement of these component mouth parts = the foundation of your ability to communicate verbally.

Your mouth, with its many functions and moving parts, is a most impressive piece of your Navigation Gear. It rates as A Deluxe Exploration Unit all its own. Taste and fuel intake... mastication... digestion aid... breathing... speaking... yelling... smiling... singing. This instrument of verbal and facial expression... with its dual sustenance functions... and respiration capabilities... the mouth is possibly the most multi-useful component on your physical instrument.

Flabby ol' lump that it appears to be... you will be charmed by the awesome function of your tongue as the receptor of that most subtle and divine of the 5 physical senses... taste. Ahhhh... Taste. Tang... sweet... salty... spice. The savor of flavor. Thru-out your incarnation, the task of taking in nourishment to sustain your physical apparatus is an ongoing endeavor. This continuous intake of nourishment would become quite tedious... boring, even... if not for the installation of these marvelous taste sensors.

Taste... making fuel intake a much more enjoyable experience.

Planet Earth is one of the 4 score planets upgraded eons ago to endow incarnate humans with the full spectrum of taste enhancers... sour and sweet... bitter and salty... tart and tangy. Sublime. And totally functional. No need to eat only crackers and water... or those boring granular protein packets. Nourishing the cellular reality of your physical body can now be varied and hugely pleasurable.

Humans have advanced a vast arena of complex culinary creativity... growing spices and herbs to add flavor to foods... cleverly combining different ingredients... making sauces... marinades... soups and stews. Devising books to share recipes. Recipes are the how-to of culinary creativity... do this... do that... add this and some of that... at 350 degrees for 30 minutes. Humans have come up with many assorted ways to "cook" food... boil... roast... sauté... blanch... bake... fry. Nuances.

You know... one must applaud the very clever move that was made along the way. Sheer insight. "Let's equip the human instrument with engaging sensory enhancements to make the repetitive requirements of biological processes more enjoyable." Brilliant. Fuel must be consumed to keep this physical apparatus alive... let's make food tasty. Reproduction must be achieved for the species to continue flourishing... let's make procreation... sexy. Arousal and deliciousness... guaranteed to engage the masses. A well-thought-out... dare I say... *ingenious* plan. Way to ensure continued success! Way to keep it all happening.

So you'll like this... your taste function will be completely harmonized with your sense of smell. Perfecto! At times... you will smell something luscious and the taste buds on your tongue will squirt little, enthusiastic bursts of saliva in joyful anticipation of taste and ingestion. You will find the flavor range of your taste sensors most enjoyable. Rather than just guzzling your fuel intake... you will learn to savor and attentively value taste... alert to and perceiving the dynamics... the aromas... the subtleties... of Earth's vast flavor spectrum. As mentioned previously... beyond the frills of pleasure... taste and smell operate together in 2 truly crucial functions: alerting you to nearby food-partaking availabilities, and warning if a fuel item has moved beyond prime to putrid. Always heed the stinky! Don't eat it.

Your Human Vehicle is particularly attractive with the thrills and sensations of its Classic 5 Senses Package. However, I feel it is my responsibility to be completely honest with you. Right now, there is one rather startling limitation to incarnating human on Planet Earth. To put it bluntly... your incarnate instrument will lack the familiar and functional Extra Sensory Perception we are all accustomed to. I know... you're right. This does seem ridiculously constricting. Believe me... we have received more than a few complaints. As entertaining as the 5 physical senses can be... I get that many of you are thinking, *Why even bother to incarnate without the usual full array of extra-sensory options?*

Here's the deal... extra-sensory perception actually *is* standard issue on the Human Vehicle. However, for many human centuries, this function has been set on "mute." Thus, these sensitivity receptors seem to be completely unavailable. In all fairness... this lack of Extra Sensory Perception within the human vehicle must be considered in context. Remember... you are incarnating human on Planet Earth. There are inherent limitations. Many incarnate humans have no clue such exceptional perception is even an item... much less that it is available to them. Others know "something is missing"... yet they cannot really identify what that something may be.

Let me offer perspective. As you may recall... one of the enticements of the human experience is to fall so deeply into it... to get sucked so deeply into density... that you sense Zero Insight Precepts (Z.I.P.). Residing shackled within the constraints of non-comprehension is simply the way Life *is* for the mass number of incarnate humans at this time. There you are, stumbling around in human form, consciously aware of Z.I.P.

Many incarnants have moments of awakened awareness. In some cases, this deep knowing sticks... lifting ongoing

Life perceptions... becoming useful. A true gift. In other cases... not so much. There can be flashes... sparkles of insight. How to sustain anything beyond a blink... a brief light show? The human involved must be fortified to the degree they are able to hang onto them insights. Many incarnate humans are simply not developed enough to carry the awakening moment to any kind of fruition.

I'll tell you, tho... when you *are* able to hang on to it... when you *do* begin to recall purpose and possibilities! This awareness enters your Life with quite a satisfying Zing! You'll find yourself reveling... "I *knew* there was more!"

These "sparkles of insight" come at a point in the human process where meditation and mindful breath can be especially helpful. Awakening is ongoing... for everyone. It begins as a process of remembering. Remembering there is more. Remembering who you are. Remembering to stop scaring yourself. Remembering to value lifting awareness. Remembering gratitude. Compassion. Kindness. Remembering your intent for incarnating.

For some, awakening comes in a flash... an epiphany... which changes their relationship with Life forever. For most... slowly, over time... awareness of the realm of extended possibilities begins to dawn. It occurs to you that Intuition and Inspiration reside beyond the limiting binds of mere Intellect.

Your early experiences in the waking-up process will actually seem pretty random… more than a little hit-or-miss. As Life goes on… little awareness sparks seem to just *happen*. Actually… you are becoming more *invested*. More consciously aware. You are drawn to explore what may not have even occurred to you before. You continue to decipher your instrument… to decode your Life experiences. All this because you *want* to. You'll have glimpses of awakening… remembering… recapitulating. These initial glimpses can turn out to be equal parts… fun… fascination… and frustration.

The moment comes. You purposely choose to awaken. "I *will* develop my awareness."

While ensconced in human circuitry… slogging thru the deep, dank density of Life on Planet Earth… your Extra Perception Options will show up as A Gift. Boy, will they ever! In time, the mute switch disengages. Your Extra Sensory Instrument awakens and develops thru your own intention and practice. New and enticing realizations. Expanded recognition of choices and capabilities.

Your sensitivity receptors are programmed to come online as you become more aware… more compassionate… more functional. Consciously having to work for this awakening gives it greater value. That is the human way. "I *want* it." Work it, Baby. Work it.

This is not a bad system. At times... it will be exasperating. Painfully limiting. You are in human form... spellbound by distraction. You will find... the process of remembering who you are... the *what* and the *why* you are... is akin to wriggling yourself out of a dulled awareness straitjacket.

Remember... you are here... now... at The Interpretorium... because you signed up for this. Because you *want to* incarnate human on Planet Earth. The fabulousness. The frustrations. The foibles. It's All simply part of The Ride. You just deal with the inherent disappointments. I know it probably sounds like I'm saying... "Get over it." Well, yeah. Pretty much, I am.

Dealing with disappointment is a significant human issue on Planet Earth. As you are currently here in the grace of complete cognition... the non-fulfillment of hopes and expectations is a foreign concept. What is fulfillment, you might ask? What is non-fulfillment? When you are human... occupied with unquenched desires... discontent attitudes... expectant emotions... dissatisfaction is a genuine struggle.

A large part of each person's struggle comes from the fact that, since early in the human incarnate cycles... for reasons I do not even pretend to understand... it has been considered a requirement to keep "secret" or "hidden" this knowledge of your truth as Soul Conscious Awareness.

Truthfully... I've always wondered... Why? What good does that actually serve? Fortunately... you are cruising into incarnation at a time when the usefulness of that whole "keep it hidden" process is being strongly questioned. And in many cases, actually dismantled.

What does this concealment procedure actually accomplish? It just slows things down even more. The already sluggish, laborious Earthtone awakening process continues dawdling along. Toddling along. On Planet Earth, that crucial process is pokey enough. Waking up takes a degree of will and intention that the "average human" does not have easy inner access to. I am happy to tell you... there is a movement in higher circles of consciousness... many of us have been petitioning for quite some time... to allow human incarnants to embody a greater sense of conscious awareness right from the get-go.

Fortunately, those of you in this particular Prep Cluster have received a matrix transformation upgrade. This allows you to reside in human form with a more effective degree of conscious awareness. Thank Goodness. It's a bold move. And it speaks well of you, being recognized for your compassionate... aware... choices... in previous human incarnations.

You are one of the first Experimental Incarnate Batches to be given this "from the get-go" awakening flex. This means certain realization furtherments are already wired into your instrument's sensory options. Listen... before you actually sign off on your human habitation license and take residence in your B.E.I.N.G.... I strongly suggest... go ahead and fill out the application for My Complete Extra-Sensory Upgrade. Just ask your Threshold Adviser for a request configuration. A favored statement on Planet Earth is, "Ask and you shall receive." That proves to be a helpful reminder.

The chances of The Extra-Sensory Upgrade just happening without you asking for it are slim. Believe me, this upgrade compliance is worth checking out. Mention that you are in this particular Incarnate Prep Cluster. I am sure that will give you dispensation to receive both... the advanced wiring harness... and your innovative software amendments. It is definitely worth your while to speak up. Request it. Tell them I sent you.

Oh, and while we're on the subject of human instrument limitations... do not anticipate shape-shifting on Planet Earth at this time. I doubt you really expected that to be available. I just want to be clear... it's not.

Alrighty, then. Let us continue familiarizing ourselves with the features that *do* currently function in your physical incarnant device. Let's move on to vision. You have been able to "see" since donning your B.E. Suit. Now you will engage some of the nuances. Your actual visual sense receptors have slipped into place. You'll notice your eyes have coverlets... your "lids." These open and close independently... allowing you to regulate the vision impulse... adjust to the intense "bright" of visual input sensation... and keep dust out of your eyes. As you begin looking around... if your head begins a sharp throb... release the coverlets to slide down over your optical globes. This will allow you to avert visual stimuli... as well as moisten and rest your eyes for a moment. When you adjust and it is comfortable for you to lift your lids... do look around. You now see each cognent operative in their individual B.E. Suit. And every "body" is seeing you in yours.

Now that you can see your fellow form units... each fleshling body... it is clear that every one has its own physical presentation. Each looks similar, yet different... just as it will be on Planet Earth. Each "person" has a different type of hair and different skin tones. You know how "The Great What Is" gets such a kick out of assortment and diversity. You also see... we have a wide variety of shapes and sizes. There are differences in height and build. Some folks are round... others are slim. Some are tall... others shorter. It's all packaging.

Look at the faces of your fellow fleshlings. Each face has structural elements... forehead at the top of the face... chin at the bottom. Cheekbones are in the middle... on either side of your nostril tote. This tote is called your *nose*. Do you notice that the plane of the face displays only four feature components? Mouth... nose... 2 eyes. Well... I guess there are 6 components... if you count the furry stripe above each eye. Even tho these components are few, each "face" is recognizably distinct... unique. Planet Earth's reputation as a cornucopia of variety is certainly apparent in the vast assortment of human appearance. None is better. None worse. Just different. Abundant physical variety is a notable feature of each planet in The "All-Skate" Alliance.

Continuing to exercise your visual sense receptors... look around at the area we are in. You will see Team Interpretorium has generated... out of replicated Earth matter... a "classroom" scenario. This is to help familiarize you with basic Planet Earth environs. In this "room" simulation... there is a ceiling above you... and a floor that everything... including you... is resting upon. Holding the ceiling and the floor at a functional distance from each other are 4 walls with several cut-in openings. These cut-ins are called windows and doors. There is opening and closing involved. Windows let air and light in. Doors are the most convenient way to get into and out of a room.

There are many rooms on Planet Earth. They, too, come in various shapes and sizes... fulfilling many different functions and activities.

You will also notice that in this room... you each are sitting in your own chair... connected to a small table with a drawer on one side. That's what that little knob is about. Pull on the knob... the drawer slides open. As you give it a slight push... it slides closed. Drawers are convenient receptacles to stash the myriad bits and pieces of human Life.

You also see that each individuated body is swathed in a smooth outer wrapper. This wrapper is made of a resilient, multi-layered cellular concoction called *flesh*. This flesh covering is your *skin*. Your skin creates your personal containment unit... making each human appear separate. Skin is amazingly pliant and quite functional. It keeps all of your organs, muscles, and fluids neatly contained. Your skin also keeps biologically harmful agents... bacteria, virus, infection... out of said organs, muscles, and fluids. Altho flesh does its job very well... it is also tender and vulnerable. Skin can be ripped, scraped, or punctured. This could allow important bodily fluids to pour out... and undesirable bacteria to enter your biological unit. Once in and under your skin... these totally tiny micro-organisms can then fester and spread. This creates ill-advised infection. Care must be taken to keep your flesh intact. This can be achieved by rubbing your skin with oils and emollients... thus keeping it supple and lubricated.

As well as being an effective bio-unit wrapper... thru-out the skin are dual-function tactile sensation components. These sensory units... nerve points... can provide you with the purely pleasurable... or warn you when something is too hot... or when your flesh wrapper is scuffed or pierced. As I am sure you are well aware... one of the definite attractions to incarnating in a human vehicle... is the delightful tactile experiences the skin provides. I would like to share one of my favorites with you now. Because you are incarnating on a water planet... what could be better than being equipt with sensory components that allow you to feel the grace of water sliding over your skin?! You are going to love this. Some would say it feels "heavenly." I am adjusting your B.E. Suit sensory components. You will feel water gently sliding over your skin. Ah, there... can you feel it?

Here, with a deft adjustment... I'll make it a little warmer. Ahhhh... Isn't that luscious? Heavenly, indeed. Okay. Now, a quick jet of cold. Ohh! Frisky!

Speaking of incarnating on a water planet... some of you have expressed frustration that your B.E.I.N.G.... as currently outfitted... will not be equipt to breathe underwater. What can I say? Like the seeming lack of Extra Sensory Capacity... being unable to breathe underwater is simply one of the human vehicle's inherent limitations. Breathing while underwater is certainly a beneficial attribute. And, yes... this ability is available on the majority of Hydration Upgrade planets. It is simply not a feature of your Earthtone vehicle. It is not going to be part of the Human Vehicle Model any time soon. You will be able to move thru water... but you'll have to come up for air. This whole skin sensory water experience... that's as close as you're gonna get. Let's face it... that in itself is a beautiful thing.

When the moment presents itself for being in and under water... look into snorkel and SCUBA gear to enhance your experience.

Now, let's move on to exploring the extremities of your B.E. Suit. Incarnating as you are... a modern human... you will be capable of bipedal locomotion as you move about the planet. There's a lot to be said about the ability to walk upright. I know you have noticed... you actually have 4 extremities. You have your 2 *arms* above... and your 2 *legs* below. Initially, as you turn your attention to these appendages, they will feel like long, heavy, limp noodles.

Due to the human body's extensive neural connective network... as you think about moving these extremities... you'll find they do, indeed, move. Somewhat slow and clunky at first... but move, they will. Take a moment to think into your arms. Give them a stretch. Pull them up above your head. Yeah, they are pretty heavy at first. Now reach them out in front of you. You will notice the highly functional bend unit... that articulation joint... mid-length in each arm. This is your *elbow*. Engage your arms... lift... bend... adjust. Wave your arms around. Waggle them to and fro. Be mindful not to make uncontrolled contact upon other bodies near you. As you are now *in* a physical body... this kind of "hit" can be quite a smack. And a source of consternation. Give your arms a few more stretches and bends. Then you can relax, and put them down.

As you are ready... think into those 2 lower appendages... your legs. As the neural network connects... stretch these legs out in front of you. This will give you a feel for their weight and length. You will notice your legs also each have a bend joint mid-length. These are your *knees*. Sitting in your chair... turn to the open side... away from the desk and drawer. Hold onto the back of your chair. This will help you balance as you stand up. Pulling the bottoms of your legs back toward your chair... bend your knee joints. Inhale deeply. As you exhale... slowly push weight onto your legs. Your knees straighten. Look at you! You are standing up!

Dizziness may occur as your head goes up several feet in elevation. Standing slowly = the operative maneuver to avoid the woozy. As you are standing... focus your thoughts to avert the sway. It will take only a few moments for the precepts of physical body balance to come back to you. I would say it's "like riding a bike"... but you're not there yet.

Your B.E.I.N.G.—Your Bio Energy Incarnate Navigation Gear

As you are in incarnation... when bike-riding time comes... you will grok my reference. Continuing to hold on to the back of your chair... engage your knee joints... practice bending your knees and lifting your legs up and down.

As you grasp the back of your chair... you have undoubtedly already discovered that your arms end in another jointed articulation unit... your *wrist*... which connects your arms to your 2 highly useful *hands*. As you are standing... from this lofty perch... venture a glance down at the floor. You will see there... at the ends of your legs... you are actually standing on 2 very functional *feet*.

The hands at the ends of your arms are the particularly well-designed, 10-digit model, with 4 fingers on each hand, thus allowing a deftness of fine-motor dexterity. The fingers on each hand come in 4 different sizes. You will be glad to see that each hand also sports a well-positioned, opposable thumb. These thumbs are the bee's knees! Well, not exactly. That is just an expression of admiration. Bee's knees don't look anything like thumbs. The installation of 1 human thumb on each hand works in concert with the 4 fingers... allowing your 5 digits to effectively grasp and handle objects.

Similar to your mouth... your hands and fingers are multi-functional Deluxe Exploration Units. You can use your hands to... wave "Hello" to your fellow humans... or grasp food and place it in your mouth. You can tickle... grip... point. There is an entire human language based on making signs with your hands and fingers. With the keratin *nails* covering one side of the tip of each finger and thumb... you will be able to scratch your skin when it itches. There's *nothing* quite as satisfying as a pesky itch getting a good scratch.

Now let's take a look at those feet. If looking down makes you dizzy... either bend your knees and return to sitting in your chair... or channel your balance to remain standing. The dizziness will pass. Observation will show... an *ankle* or bending joint at the end of each leg. This creates a 90-degree angle between your leg and your foot. Your foot is what you actually stand and walk on. Just as each hand has 5 digits... 4 fingers and a thumb... each foot has 5 *toes*. These, too, each come tipped with a keratin nail. Toes come in 5 sizes... one large... one tiny... 3 sizes in between. Unless specially trained... toes are not particularly adept at picking up items or tossing things. Toes' claim to fame? They are all about sustaining upright balance, which leads to walking... running... skipping... dancing. As a bipedal human, you will find those little digits down there supremely helpful.

Let's take a few moments to experiment with walking. If you are sitting, please stand. Until you gain confidence... you can hold onto the back of your chair and walk around your desk. The back area of your foot, directly under the ankle, is your *heel*. Your walking step begins by putting weight on your heel... rolling forward along your foot... until your weight is over your toes. Lift and propel your other leg several inches ahead and again... weight on heel... roll on thru... finish with toes. Now move your other leg on thru. You'll catch on quickly. As you get the hang of balance and propulsion... bipedal locomotion is not that complicated. Those of you who are still holding onto your chair... as you feel confident... let go. Launch. Isn't that sweet... feeling your balance and motion coordinating as you practice this activity of forward mobility? Walk around the room. Try not to hold on to anything. No! Wait! Not even the wall!

After practicing forward stepping... if you really want to change things up... move one foot back behind you. Execute some backward steps. Does that sound a little too wild? It may be easier than you think. There are times when the ability to smoothly walk backward may come in handy.

In the course of your incarnate experience, you will likely learn to dance. Dance is a physical body art form of rhythmic movement... frequently accompanied by music and a beat. Dance has been significant in the human experience for eons. There are myriad and fabulous different ways to dance. There is also hopping... skipping... jumping...

and jive. Some dance is ceremonial and structured. Some dance is loose and free-form. Dance celebrates locomotion in a whole different realm. You'll love it!

To be kept in mind... the human incarnant package comes in one of two different containment units. You will either be female... a girl, then a woman... or male... a boy, then a man. As you birth in your Navigation Gear... based on your own karmic overtones... you will already be equipt as either female or male. Either is a worthwhile experience. One is not better nor worse... not greater nor lesser... than the other. Each has a wide variety of functions and roles to play. As customs and practices on Planet Earth have developed over time... it currently appears that females play a subservient role to males. This is both misleading and unfortunate. Much of the strife... lack... and misalignment... that is rampant in this planetary realm... is a direct result of this fateful imbalance between male and female.

As the biologics of the Human Resilience Project continue to unfold on Planet Earth... both male and female units are required to perpetuate the species for further experimentation. Men plant the seed containing their genetic material. Women meet that seed with an egg and contribute their own biological characteristics. Women are equipt with the womb that grows the new incarnant(s). The vast majority of times... women are the ones who nurture... sustain... and train the new being thru the rigors of childhood development.

Humans... stewing in their oddly limited View of All Things... place a much greater emphasis than is realistic or necessary on whether you're a girl or a boy. All sorts of narratives and attitudes have developed as to why it is better to be one or the other. There is surprising rancor... miscommunication... even the pain of mistrust... between human men and women. This to the point that the common wisdom on both sides is... "Can't live with 'em. Can't live without 'em." You'll easily see what I mean when you get there.

Let's take a break now. That means doing something different for a while. You will be standing up and walking out of this room thru a door. This will give you an opportunity to seek nourishment, sustenance and fluids to nurture the well-being of your B.E. Suit. Outside this room, you will find directions to the Food Court, where there will be many different fuel and beverage options.

We're all about making your B.E. Suit simulation as authentic as possible. In conjunction with this classroom setting... and the replicated oxygen-rich "air" of Planet Earth... we have modeled physical body capacities to allow you a comprehensive experience of the biological functions of the human instrument. With that in mind... lavatories or "rest rooms" are located down the hall.

CHAPTER 3

Fluency

*"Meditation expands and articulates...
far beyond anything you could have first imagined."*

I've mentioned before... as I began studying The Nature of The Soul, the concept that fascinated me the most was that we humans operate in our world thru 3 bodies... physical, emotional, and mental. And that our Spiritual body... our essence... interpenetrates and animates all 3 of our other bodies.

Sure, I knew we had a physical body, and that everybody has feelings and emotions. And we all certainly do think, think, and think. It had not occurred to me that my feelings are my "emotional body"... or my thoughts are my "mental body." And... just as we live in a physical environment... we all also live in an "emotional environment" and a "mental environment." Interacting with our world... as we express in our physical environment... we're also affected by, and have an effect within, our emotional environment and our mental environment.

Considering my "instrument" this way caused me to experience my thoughts and emotions differently. Stimulated by my growing awareness of my emotional self and my mental instrument, I began to see… it is a worthwhile endeavor to "get a handle on" my thoughts and feelings. To delve into what motivates me... and what limits me. To become familiar with and more at ease within my own "ways and means."

"Ways and means" can be defined as... "the methods and resources at a person's disposal to achieve something." Including the spiritual body, our 4 bodies are our "methods and resources" as we walk our Path and interact with our world.

Sitting there in The Nature of The Soul class in my early 20s, I was aware that I did not always "achieve something" I set out to do. I had zero understanding of why or how that was. It hadn't occurred to me I could be undermining or sabotaging my own self.

What kept me from following thru on my ideas and intentions? Truthfully, let's word that more accurately... How did I keep myself from following thru on my intentions? How did I undermine and misguide myself? Did *I* mentally or emotionally keep myself from accomplishing my intentions and from attaining my goals? How was I tying my shoelaces together at the beginning of the race?

As I mentioned in Chapter 1, when I was a child, I used to wonder, *What is it that "leaves" when a person dies?* I thought about this a lot. You might wonder, how is it a kid even thinks about stuff like that? Well, here's why... my father would take me out of school to attend funerals with him. Funerals of his friends or coworkers... rarely people I knew. Sitting in the chapel or standing graveside gave me many an occasion to wonder about "what leaves?" The deceased person's physical body is still there. But, obviously, "they" aren't. What left?

Clarifying that for me... The Nature of The Soul explained that we are animated by a Spiritual Essence... our Soul Consciousness. This is what "leaves" when we die. We humans are more than the sum of our physical, emotional, and mental parts. It is the animating spark of Spirit that keeps it all a'movin' and a'groovin'. Without that spark... that animating inner essence... these bodies of ours simply fall right over. They lose their stuff. As that essence...

our crucial vitalizing content... leaves... all the other parts disincorporate. Dissolve. Return to dust. That animating force is the fascinator. Fascinating to be aware of... to delve into. To find to be an ally. This Life force fascinates us into existence. Equally fascinating: a person can live a whole Life without being aware that they... and the choices they make... are animated by their Soul Conscious Awareness.

Self-revelation seeps in as my awareness of my 3 bodies increases. I had not once thought about being completely "present"... all of myself being in this current moment. I'd never considered how "I" might be in *this* place in my physical body... while my thoughts... my mental body... is off fully engaged somewhere else. I'm sitting *here* but my mind is far away... thinking about my morning commute... or last year's trip to Italy... or my 5th grade piano recital.

Then there's the question of what I am *feeling* in this moment. Totally unrelated to where I actually am and what I'm doing... I could be sitting here feeling upset by the rude remark some guy made yesterday... or angry about having to re-do the project I've been working on... or I could be totally anxiety-absorbed about meeting my hot date tomorrow night. What I'm thinking and feeling have nothing to do with where I actually am. Instead of being here, now... I am there, then. Basically... anywhere but here.

A greater understanding of myself and my relationship with my 3 bodies began to dawn on me. In this moment... I *could* be completely present... integrated mentally, emotionally, physically. I began to realize how personally incongruent I was. As I developed my ability to observe my thoughts and emotions, I found... Woo Boy!... I was scattered all over the place! *Crazy* scattered. Everywhere else but here. What about being totally attentive where I am? Ha! My thoughts *could* be engaged with what I'm doing right now. My emotional energy centered... present where I am. It's a fascinating concept to entertain. I began giving more authentic attention to where I am... what I'm thinking... what I'm feeling. *Am I all "here?" Or am I entertaining myself in the vast, chattering multi-plex of my past? Or speculating about what my future may bring?*

Altho I did not see it in my early 20s... looking back at my Life now, I realize I had a natural propensity for the information and training I received thru The Nature of The Soul. I drank it up. Like a person parched being handed a cool, refreshing glass of limeade. I hadn't realized how thirsty I was. The information about our 3 bodies simply made sense. It woke up a knowing in me. Of course, we are physical, emotional, mental beings animated by a spark of consciousness. Of course, we are.

Evidently, I came hard-wired with a fluency for this quality of understanding. Since my teens... I have been aware that I "came in with the door half open." I have always heard "voices." When Scott and I first met, he was working in the field of mental health. When I told him I heard voices, he said, "Dana, you do realize that is a sign of mental illness?" I responded, "It all depends on what the voices are telling you."

One of my best "voices" spoke to me now and again thruout my childhood. Randomly, it would say, "Remember what this feels like." During my teens... perhaps to clarify the point... the voice elaborated... "Remember what this feels like, because you are going to be on the other side of it." I knew this referred to being a parent. I raised my 2 miraculous children "remembering what it felt like" to be a child, especially a teenager. For this, I am most grateful. It worked well for all of us.

I have had past-Life recall my whole Life. It did not occur to me that other people didn't. My first clear recollection: I was 5 years old, sitting on the hill in our backyard watching the new neighbors move in next-door. As I watched the man walking around, I was aware that I had known him before. I remember giving myself examples... I have known him before like I have known Grandma before. (My deep connexion with my Grandmother, whom

I saw only a handful of times in my Life, is a whole other story.) I thought of my Aunt Lucy Ruth. More examples of other people "I've known before" came into my 5-year-old mind. On this same day... there was a moment when the new neighbor, Ken, came thru the door at the back of his garage wearing unusual clothes (in my mind's eye). I watched him walk around the side of his garage in this "outfit." Several years later, watching the movie *Ben Hur*, I saw what the Roman soldiers wore and thought, "Oh, that's what Ken was wearing the day they moved in." Coming out of his garage that day, I saw Ken dressed as a Roman soldier. (Again, this was in my mind's eye. Obviously, Ken was not actually moving into his new house wearing a Roman soldier costume.) This wonderful man and his dear wife, Irma, lived next door to my parents for more than 50 years. The 2 couples were great friends. All these years... Ken has been and still is a treasured part of my Life... a very dear friend.

Growing up, I did not realize that I was "wired" any differently than anyone else. When you're a kid, you think everyone's thoughts... their interests... their home-life... are just like yours. When I was 15, I heard the word "reincarnation" for the first time. My first response... "Oh good, there's a word for it." It did not strike me as odd or even "special" that I would have recall experiences... or that I sometimes knew about things before they happened. As I was moving thru my Life… this was just "the way things are."

I am ever-grateful for the grace and dimensionality this awareness gives my Life.

Over the years, it has become clear to me that you "mature" as a human being as you take responsibility for your Life. This means taking responsibility for the Life you are living and the effect you and your Life have on others. *Response-ability.*

Muddling thru Life, we humans seem wired (would this be "nature" or "nurture"?) to believe "it" is always someone else's fault. Whatever "it" might be. *Why am I so miserable? What is this messed up concoction that is my Life? Who's to blame here? Not me! All of these dismal instances I call my Life are somebody else's fault… my dad… my 4th grade teacher… my coach… that lousy co-worker… neighbor… boss… ex-lover. I certainly would not have made this mess myself!*

At times, the thought of "taking responsibility for my Life" can be terrifying. Beyond overwhelming. But, as they say… if not you, who? Fatefully followed by… if not now, when? As long as you believe any situation or feelings you have are "someone else's fault"… you hold yourself as the "victim." And you give the other person(s) undeserved power over you.

Realize you are accountable… for your actions… your words… your thoughts… your reactions. This isn't accountable in a harsh, austere way. This is accountable in a "You *Get To* Do This!" way. Realizing you are accountable hands you the reins… gives *you* the power to do something about it. You *can* transform your Life. I'm not saying it's easy. It's pretty complex. But, I am here to tell you… it is totally worthwhile.

As with so many aspects of Life… delving into the reality of personal response-ability… you will find that you activate undercover field-agents busy operating from your past, your present, and your future. There are tenacious tentacles from your past choices (conscious or unconscious) and beliefs (conscious or unconscious) that are affecting… coloring… possibly even consuming… your Life as it is now.

Disentangling from long-standing circumstances and unhealthy relationships takes:

1. intention
2. attentive awareness
3. perseverance.

With as little self-judgment as possible… you set about cleaning your inner house. Taking a good look at "stuff." Tidying up… moving things around… tossing and recycling. Instigating change. You make conscious decisions. You look at your Life with the open eyes of how you want it to be. Not blindly continuing to stumble along in the habit of things as they have been.

Changing your thoughts about who you are and how your Life can be has a transforming effect on how your Life is. You are the author of your own existence. The poet of your perception. And your pain. What do you tell yourself about who you are and what your Life is? "I have a good Life." "My Life sucks." "Of course, I can do this!" "Why even try?" What you see is what you get. Your inner narrator is constantly telling you the story of who you are and what this Life you are living is all about.

As far as your present and your future... you take huge steps in the direction of personal response-ability when you realize you can respond rather than react to the experiences Life tosses your way. This is conscious choice. Enormous choice. Every experience we interact with offers an opportunity to continue developing the ability to *respond* to what is happening... rather than just automatically *react* to it. Reacting and responding offer you 2 very different ways of dancing with the players and circumstances in your Life.

Reaction is a reflex... a minion of unconscious being. Without you even realizing... reaction snaps up the moment with the ol' "I've always done it this way and I always will." No options required. And none offered... to yourself... nor to the situation. Knee-jerk reaction to conditions and circumstances offers you no choice... no possibilities. This is usually powered by troubled emotion... and the misbelief: "I

Fluency

have no choice." Snap! Your "react!" keeps you right where you've always been. And, you know what? Many times, that "snap to" reaction makes things even worse.

As you respond, you come from a greater awareness of options. Responding means you have given yourself a moment to be *awake* in the midst of what is going on or what is being said. What *is* going on? What *is* being said? As you respond... you contribute... you interact in a way that could actually bring something fresh... something positive... to the moment. This is you being competent with yourself. Being competent with your world.

Reacting is an automatic reflex that "has you." It grabs you. It snaps you up. You react without awareness. Reaction lives in the unconscious realm that depends upon... "She made me do it!" "This is the way I gotta be." "Don't make me think about the way I mindlessly flail about in my Life." "I can't let him get away with this!" "I don't have a choice." Funny thing about choice... when you believe you have no choice... you're right... you don't. Choice is only an option when you open the door to let it in.

As you choose to respond... you can take a moment to draw a deep, centering breath. That's allowed. Even in the midst of the whoop-dee-doo. There's nothing in the "rulebook" that says... "must plow ahead"... "take no time to be mindful." Sometimes, you do get snagged... pulled along... reacting. As soon as you realize you're crashing thru the reacting briar patch again... there is *no* "rule" saying you can't... in that moment... stop action and draw a deep breath. And give yourself a moment to respond. There is context... there are options... and there are consequences to consider. Respond differently this time. Change it up. Mindfulness rocks. Especially right in the midst of thorny interactions.

Let's face it, that knee-jerk reaction is what gets us in trouble. As heated, bristly words are exchanged... your unthinking reaction can pour gasoline on the fire. The situation combusts. The other person ignites... becomes defensive... reacts... burns on. And there it all goes... erupting out of control.

This cyclone of misunderstanding can be re-routed as you make the choice... to draw a deep breath... consider your response... and maybe even try to understand what the other person is attempting to communicate. You do not need to be the victim of your knee-jerk reactions. You can choose to respond. You can be present in *this* moment, too.

Realizing that you have 3 bodies and the ability to do something about them is instrumental in making Life-aware choices. Realizing that your emotional nature is not The Boogie Man is really helpful, too. We humans are so afraid of our emotions. So afraid of ourselves. Developing a kind, compassionate relationship with your own fine self takes you giant steps in the direction of psychological good health and personal well-being. This is the result of conscious choice. You make a conscious decision to be more self-aware... even if, at first, you hear yourself saying... "I don't know what that even means."

As I've mentioned, when I began meditating, I had no idea what meditation *was*... and it came as a surprise to me that there are many different ways to meditate. As it turns out, there are also many different *whys* to meditate.

Let's say you have 10 people standing in front of you who each consider themselves to be a meditator. You ask them... "What is meditation? Why do you meditate?" Chances are real good you will get 10 completely different responses. One person might say, "I meditate to relax my body. I mindfully go thru and release tension, relaxing the muscles in each part of my body. As I meditate, I visualize myself succeeding in my physical pursuits. This gives me strength and focus to excel in my physical body."

Another meditator might say, "I meditate to calm my emotions. Over time, I've developed centered guidance as I go thru the many aspects of my emotional self to find a place of deep and certain peace." One reason you might hear is, "My religion tells me to meditate, so I do." Another person could say, "I meditate to quiet the chatter in my mind, to disentangle from my incessant over-think. I meditate to clear my mind and quiet my thoughts." Another would say, "My relationship with Spirit is important to me. As I practice meditation, my connexion with Spirit blossoms and thrives." Each of these different "reasons" to meditate is right and true.

As I practiced TM's mantric meditation, I didn't give a moment's thought to whether there were other ways to meditate. Stumbling into meditation as I did... I didn't know there was anything "else" to think about. Turns out, there are many ways to meditate. If you are just beginning to consider meditation, check out and experiment with different meditation forms. Find the one that hums for you. As soon as you begin exploring... you are building your relationship with meditation. Continuing to investigate... explore... contemplate... you will establish your own meditation practice.

Perhaps you have found a way to meditate that feels right to you. Stick with it. You can deepen into meditation with the guidance of a teacher or guru... or you can find your way on your own. You establish your own relationship with meditation... thru your interest... your own engaged search... your practice.

Establish the habit of meditation in your daily Life.

Thru the years, so many people have said to me... "I know I should meditate." And yet for a variety of reasons, they don't let themselves. #1 Most Frequently Heard Reason for "Why I can't meditate": "I can't quiet my thoughts." Yep, it's a wild cacophony in there. "The chatter in my head is relentless." They don't call it monkey-mind for nothin'. "Every time I've tried to meditate, I just give up. My thoughts are too noisy." And so it is... for *everybody*. Has ever a human sat to meditate for the first time and met with sublime absence of chatter? I don't know. I'm thinking probably not. We're human... we chatter.

Ultimately, the question is, "Who's going to win here... you... or the incessant chatter?"

Let's say you've decided to take on that chatter. You are going to start meditating. Any new undertaking brings up, "I don't know what I'm doing." And that's okay. Simply proceed. With your interest and intent you are, in fact... building... welcoming... composing... your meditation practice.

Your practice can be... *should* be... designed in a way that serves you best. If you feel at a loss as to how to proceed... ask somebody you know who meditates to recommend possibilities. Google... "meditating"... "meditation"... "mindfulness." Look for meditation books, CDs, apps, or classes.

Living as we do in The Age of A Gajillion Resources... don't let yourself be duped by that old stand-by... "I don't know how."

There is no good reason to allow your doubt and resistance to tie your shoelaces together at the beginning of the race.

The important thing is to meditate. Just do it. At least once a day is ideal. When possible... it's good to meditate at the same time each day... and, if you can... in the same place. We humans are a rhythmic lot. The rhythm of meditating at the same time each day will serve you well. That said... if your Life does not allow you to meditate at the same time... don't let that be an excuse to not meditate. Just make time to meditate. Sometimes it takes a hammer and chisel to carve out that time. But hey... chisel away. You're worth it.

Decades ago, I came across the concept... as you meditate in the same place each day... you build an "etheric temple." The forces are drawn together... allowing you to more readily ease into your inner meditative space. If it works in your Life... it's a lovely thing to create an "altar" in your home. So many variations on that theme. A certain chair or meditation pillow. A small table in a special place. Or a whole room. You can also employ a "portable etheric temple"... have a zafu, a meditation pillow, or a prayer rug ready. Wherever you may be... as you unroll your rug or sit on your pillow... Ahhh... there you are. If your Life is such that you make time to meditate at work or school... you could always sit on the same bench... or under the same tree... or in the same bathroom stall... or in your car. Find your spot.

The bottom line: Do not let your resistance win. Don't fall for: "I don't know how to meditate." Or the ever-popular: "My thoughts are too noisy to meditate." Why should either of these self-limiting beliefs get to win? You are... after all... You. (Aka... the one in charge here.) You can *do* this.

As I mentioned... I was in college when I began studying The Nature of The Soul. At that time, the school was called San Fernando Valley State College... now it's known as CSUN or Cal State Northridge. Even when I was there in the early 70s, it was a very large school. If you did not get there early in the morning... the parking lots filled up... and there you were... parked out in the boonies = far, far away. In the afternoon, you'd be trudging way out to your car... on the hot asphalt... lugging tons of books... in the broiling sun... or pouring rain. It didn't take me many times of doing that to realize... *I could get up super early... pull myself together... drive to the school parking lot, and get a spot close in.* Parked... I'd then sit in my car and meditate. Yes, there it was... my personal "etheric temple"... in the front seat of my old black, beetle-back, stick-shift Volvo. I still remember the odd, musty interior smell. It makes me smile. And, yes, I did feel especially clever... getting myself a good parking spot... *and* having plenty of time to meditate each morning. It *is* the little things.

You may wonder... wasn't it distracting, meditating in my car in the parking lot? Well... yes, it was. Car doors slamming... people's voices... engines revving... the smell of exhaust. And yet, part of meditation practice itself is to establish a centered focus that persists... beyond being disturbed by pesky distractions. It's all exercise. Drawing another deep breath... a car door slams... loud voices... coming back to center... focusing. As I chose not to let distraction win... I was building my meditation muscles.

Truth be told... in those days, sitting in my car, a lot of what I focused on in meditation was, "Please make me happy." "I want to be happy." "Could you work it out so I could be happy?" "Please?"

When I was first teaching The Nature of The Soul... I would say to the students... "Meditate daily." Meditating daily was the way I'd been taught and how I established my own meditation practice. For me, as a young teacher, daily was "the way you do it." Then, I got older... and more "involved" with the involvements of Life. Students would complain about being "too busy." I changed "Meditate daily" to "Meditate regularly." Trying to be accommodating... meditate "when you can." But you know what? It really is best to meditate daily. Establishing a habit of daily meditation serves you well. You *can* give that to yourself. Again, I will mention… you're worth it.

It is called a meditation "practice" for a reason. As you practice… you build your meditation muscles… your capacity and capabilities. Some people meditate for a week or a month and then give up because it "didn't do anything." If you decided to learn to play the piano… you would not realistically anticipate that within a month, you would go from learning scales to playing a concerto. It doesn't happen that way. Learning something new takes time and attentiveness. You practice. You develop your skills. When you are serious about learning piano… you play the piano daily. As you learn to speak another language… you learn vocabulary… grammar… syntax. You practice speaking that language. You exercise those muscles to become fluent. Meditation is the same way. You practice to develop fluency.

Meditation is to your Spiritual Body as exercise is to your physical body. As you practice, you build your muscles. You develop your skills. You put forth. Exertion. Attention. Effort. You do this:

1. to do what you say you want to do
2. to become how you want to be
3. to establish your meditation practice
4. to absorb the Life-changing benefits of meditation

What you give your attention to is what thrives in your Life.

It took me a while to realize this Fascinating Thing about these lives we live. Look at what's Large in your Life. Fashion and make-up? Civil War reenactments? Culinary creativity? Running? Video games? What's Large is large because that's what you give your attention to. There are aspects of your Life that are "small" or "under-developed." Communicating with your parents. Housekeeping. Reading that pile of books. Walking on the treadmill. Keeping in touch with old friends. These are things you might think about doing... but you don't really give your time and attention to them. The different facets of your Life are "fed" as they receive your attentiveness. The shriveled aspects of your Life are literally starved for your attention.

Allowing meditation to become a part of your world requires a certain degree of attentiveness. Not that meditation is so "hard"... or asks "so much." But because you deserve to attend to and exercise this Life-transforming aspect of your self.

Whatever you might think meditation is as you begin meditating... it will reveal itself to be so much more. Over time... as you practice... meditation expands and articulates... far beyond anything you could have first imagined. The gifts of meditation are vast and profound. These gifts blossom before you... revealing themselves. Revealing yourself to you.

Of all the different ways to meditate I've experienced... I am still most partial to the approach I learned thru The Nature of The Soul. It makes complete sense to me to begin a meditation session by attending to this vehicle I inhabit. This "preparation phase" can take anywhere from 5 to 15 minutes... as I draw a deep, mindful breath and consciously relax my physical body. I calm and balance my emotions. I quiet and focus my mind. Then I am in a centered... attentive space... to lift... expand... open. I align with my Greater Awareness... my Soul Consciousness. I open my mind. I open my heart. I open my identity. In a whole new way.

I allow the meditation to meditate me.

Truth be told... if you have not had actual experience meditating... you do yourself a disservice by believing you know what meditation is. Meditating is so much more than thinking about meditating.

The experience of meditation is trans-dimensional... and beyond. It is challenging to put "It All" into the flat, angular boxes of words. People who have not experienced meditation... might hear or read words about meditating, and think what they think. They believe they "understand" what is being said. Whereas, folks who are experienced meditators would hear or read the same words only to realize and recognize something totally other... a knowing beyond the words conveyed.

As with every thing... *experience* conveys meaning. Articulating a fluency of content... and context. Deeper understanding. Realization.

If you are interested in meditating right now... the following experience of Mindful Breath will give you that opportunity.

The key to meditating and to Mindful Breath is to give the *experience* to yourself. And give your self to the experience. Skimming along on the surface will give you a skimming-along-on-the-surface experience. That's not what you're looking for. You get what you give. Put yourself *in* it. Allow yourself to be attentive. Present. Mindful. Absorbed.

Over the years... in my exploration and experience with meditation... I've come to realize that Mindful Breath has to be the first meditation technique we humans figured out. In many ways, it continues to be "the best." Mindful Breath does everything meditation "should do." And it's simple:

1. Your breath is always with you. How convenient is that? Totally convenient.
2. You don't have to buy anything or go anywhere to find the perfect meditation accessory. You've already got it. You *are* it.
3. Inhale and exhale right where you are.

4. Mindful Breath gives you an excellent way to focus your attention.
5. Here is your perfect opportunity to "change channels"… should your "channels" need changing… or your attitude "adjusted."
6. You can practice Mindful Breath Any Where.
7. Relaxing and restorative. Mindful Breath calms and centers you.
8. Added bonus… you disentangle from monkey-mind chatter.
9. There are myriad more reasons.
10. I could go on.

The real kicker to Mindful Breath is the "Mindful" part of it. "All you do" is give your attention to The Sweet Breath of Life as it moves in and out of your body. You ride on the rhythm of your breath.

As you inhale, focus on your breath flowing into your body. Follow with your mind as your lungs fill. As you exhale… follow your breath up thru your throat… feel it in the back of your nose… down thru your nostrils as your breath flows out. Consciously.

Choose time and again to keep your attention with your breath. Of course your mind will wander. That's what minds do. Each time you notice your thinkery has wandered away from focus on your breath… choose to bring yourself back.

Follow your next breath. Do not fuss at yourself because your mind has wandered. Fussing at yourself is only more distraction.

Ok, so probably you are already well-aware... but here I'll just say it... when you first sit to focus on your breath... you will be *Blown Away* by how Totally NOT Quiet your head is. OMG! Can it get any noisier? A Royal Cacophony! The chatter... incessant. It's not just you. Everybody's inner jibber-jabber jibs and jabs on and on. And on. Many people... awash in their unrelenting inner chatter say... "I can't meditate." Ahhhh... misperception. A wily trap too easy to dive into.

Over time... as you practice meditation or mindful breath... you develop your ability to focus. You ease yourself away from the relentless magnet of monkey-mind. You come to realize... I don't have to just hand my attention over to every pesky inner sound bite.

If everyone could immediately sit down to a centered, mindful meditation... we'd all be Buddha.

Success takes exercise.

Choice. Practice.

Success is you saying, "I can do this."

"I am doing this."

Whether you are a seasoned meditator or you are beginning your meditation practice, Mindful Breath is your Great Friend and Reliable Ally.

Mindful Breath is a magnificent way to "collect" yourself. This simple act of following your breath allows you to bring your many scattered bits to a quiet, centered place inside. The mind chatters and wanders. That's not "you" chattering and wandering. It's your thinkery.

Take a moment to listen to the chatter in your mind. It is perpetually taking you into the past. "I should have told her." "I wish I'd done it." "If only I had." Or it's taking you into the future... "When I arrive, I'm going to..." "Then I'll wear my red scarf..." "When will I ever get to... "

Past... Future. Future... Past. There it is... your inner chatter... keeping you anywhere but here.

Our untamed thinkery skitters and prattles. It's easy to understand why Buddhists call it "monkey mind." As you give yourself the gift of Mindful Breath... the great wandering mind is called again and again to join you in *this* moment. In *this* breath. You know... the breath you are breathing right now is really the only breath. Just as this *is* the only moment. You can't breathe again your most recent breath. You can't breathe your next breath. You can only breathe this breath.

Stay with your breath as you inhale deeply... mindfully. YOU are choosing. To bring your self... your awareness... your attention... right to where you are on the planet. Right here. Right now.

Mindful in this moment... you call your skittering thoughts back from the far-flung, fabrications of "there" and "then."

Let's extend our visit with Mindful Breath... and broaden our practice.

When you choose to experience this practice... sit comfortably with your eyes closed. Focus your attention in the center of your chest. This is your heart chakra. Feel yourself "take up residence" in the center of your heart. With a deep inhale and exhale... give yourself a moment to be present in your loving, grateful heart. From this point of focus, turn your mindful attention to your breath. Inhale... slowly, deeply. Exhale... releasing completely.

As you inhale... place your attention with your breath as it enters your nostrils. With your mind... follow this breath up thru your nostrils to the top of your nose... to the back of your throat... then down your throat... filling your lungs. When your lungs are full... feel yourself begin to release. The breath leaves your lungs... comes back thru your throat... down your nostrils... releasing out into your world.

Practicing Mindful Breath... I find it very helpful to add a "beat" at the top of each movement in the cycle. Inhale deeply... as your lungs are full... hold for one beat. Then exhale. Releasing completely... hold for one beat... before

Fluency

you again inhale. This "beat" is a great assist in your mind's ability to stay focused on your breath. The "beat" gives your mind a "device" to keep your thinkery more engaged in the process. Sometimes, you just have to get tricky with your own fine self.

Your mind will wander. It's a mind... it wanders. Each time you find your mind has wandered, simply return to your breath. Your next breath is always there... here. You know your mind will wander... taking you out of this room... into the past... into the future. Anywhere but here. Here's the trick... when you notice your mind has wandered... simply return to your breath. Bring your conscious focus back to your Heart Chakra in the center of your chest. Proceed wherever you are in the inhale-exhale cycle. Your mind will wander again. When you notice your thoughts have wandered off... simply return to your breath.

Your key to success... Do not fuss at yourself when your mind wanders.

Oh, how we do fuss. It comes so naturally. So easy to succumb to. In no way is that fussing the ally it pretends to be. Fussing at yourself is simply distraction. Painful. Not self-respecting. Oh, so many variations on that theme. Release yourself from fuss. Just stop. You don't have to get all mad at yourself because your mind has wandered off... again. Do you hear yourself fussing? Don't fall for it. Grab your attention. Put it on your next breath. Proceed. No muss. No fuss.

When you begin practicing Mindful Breath, choose an amount of time you want to stay with your breath. You could start with 5 minutes... or 10... or 2. Set some sort of gentle sounding device to let you know when 5 minutes has passed. Don't think... "I'll just look at the clock." That keeps your thinkery engaged... "Is it time yet?" Also, best not to think, "I'll count breaths." That, too, keeps your thinking engaged... counting... waiting... anticipating. Thinking.

When you find yourself feeling frustrated with your mind chattering so much... or that you're not "doing it right"... simply let go of that, too. Do not fall prey to the distractions of doubt and self-judgment. That frustration is just more fuss. Do not succumb. Do not give in to the abstractions... the gyrations... the bouncing... all over the map. This is the unbridled, wild stallion of your over-think.

As you choose to return your focus to your breath... you are taking control of your mental gyrations. You are grabbing the reins. You are directing the show. If only for a moment. You are choosing peace. You are choosing center. You are choosing here... now.

And then you choose again.

Here is an option that can add dimensionality to your practice of Mindful Breath. Choose an uplifting phrase or mantra which you affirm to yourself as you ride on the rhythm of your breath. Inhale... "I am peace." Feel yourself filling with peace. As you exhale... "I release all that is not peace." Experience yourself consciously letting go of all within you that is not peace. Rinse and repeat.

Inhale... "I am confident." Exhale... "I release all that is not confidence." Don't just mindlessly repeat the words. Give yourself the experience of what you are asserting and what you are releasing.

Inhale... "I am love." Exhale... "I release all that is not love." Create your own mantra to draw in positive, affirming energy. As you exhale... release yourself from self-imposed limitation.

A variation on including mantra with your mindful breath... inhale... "I am peace." As you exhale... pour peace into your world. Inhale... "I am love." As you exhale... pour love into your world.

Mindful breath can be well-applied right in the midst of the "real world." Let's say you are at work and things get "jammed up"... many possible variations on that theme. A sour conversation with a coworker. Way too much on your plate. Your boss is being a jerk. Give yourself a moment to... if possible... get away to the aforementioned bathroom stall. Here in your "private space"... sit on the throne. Close your eyes. Give yourself a few moments to focus on Mindful

Breath. The trick, of course, is to actually give yourself the "mindful" part. You can't just quickly... sniff... blow... sniff... blow... grabbing a few distracted breaths, still tangled up in the game. It doesn't work that way.

Let go of the chatter around whatever has you triggered. Drop the poo. Ride with your breath. Give yourself a few minutes to clear... calm... center. Let go.

Then re-engage. As you return to the arena of your Life... you will be in a different place inside yourself. This can have a clarifying effect on the proceedings. If you're really on the fly and the bathroom stall is out of the question... draw a centered breath or 3 right where you are. Give yourself a nanosecond to disengage... from what's going on outside of you... and, most especially, from what's going on inside of you. Still the torrent of inner chatter. If only for a second. Connect with a clear place inside and proceed. This obviously applies anywhere... at home, immersed in the chaos of kids... or parents... or roommates. Find the bathroom. Shut the door. Sit down for a moment. Breathe. Let go. Breathe. Center. Breathe. Emerge. Re-engage. Party on.

I know I have said, "simply" choose... "simply" let go... "simply" return to your breath. The truth is, most of these conscious choices are totally simple. That does not make them totally easy. Oh, how we do like our "easy." Because I like words... I like to look them up. Dictionary or thesaurus... either works for me. I appreciate the fine nuances. In this case... "simple" means "not involved or complicated." "Easy" is defined as "posing no difficulty." So, these conscious choices and actions are "not complicated." Just do it. However... the "doing it" can "pose some difficulty"... struggling, as we often do, with our own internal resistance.

Each time you realize you are struggling with yourself... you are offered an excellent opportunity to take a look at your resistance. What am I resisting? Why?

Resistance is sly, slithering self-limitation. Resistance lurks in the dark, slippery rocks under your threshold of conscious awareness. Masquerading as a "helper"... keeping you "safe." Resistance is not the ally it pretends to be.

Many times, we don't even realize we're "resisting." That wily resistance. We seldom know why we resist. But with oh, so many things... resist we do. ("I don't want to do it.") We oppose ourselves. ("That takes too much effort.") Why do we oppose the changes in our Life we say we want? ("In this case... is my resistance actually serving me well?")

Note to self: Resistance does not always have to win. Just because I find myself resisting doesn't mean I can't give myself what I want. Be glad when you are able to see your resistance. Up until the very moment you become aware of your resistance... it "has" you. As soon as you can see it... you "have" it. Once you see your resistance... it can no longer hide. It can no longer slither. No longer can it undermine as effectively as it used to. When you become aware you are resisting, you can say, "Oh, that's just my resistance. It's not going to win this time." Then just keep on keepin' on.

This makes me think of my earlier analogies related to establishing your meditation practice... playing the piano or learning a new language. Some things in Life are definitely worth the effort. In this case the "Worth It" is *You*.

The important thing as you begin to sculpt your meditation practice is to find what works for you... what you can do that actually has you practicing meditation.

Some beginning meditators ask me about meditating with music. When I began meditating, it was without music. I can tell you... yes... at times it can be distractingly too quiet. As you begin your meditation practice... if music serves you well... then I say, use it. You can decide in the future if you want to continue meditating with music... or not. If music is something that will help you ease into your meditation practice... then, yes... meditate to music.

In this case... a few suggestions:

1. Choose music that is "plain"... "Zen"... not too melodic. Soothing music will help your mind settle... rather than jump around, "caught" by melody.

2. Use the same music each time you sit. In "knowing what to expect" your mind is soothed and will relax more deeply... rather than being engaged... "hooked"... listening to new, different sounds.
3. You might hum with the music... mindfully. Give attention to the vibration of the hum... how it feels in your chest... your throat... mouth... nose... your ears. Give attention to your breath as it "propels" your hum. And as you draw breath in... replenishing. Foam ear plugs can enhance this hum practice.

You can focus on Mindful Breath as you listen to music. This can be your beginning meditation practice. Put on some soothing music. Sit. Close your eyes. Focus in your heart center. Inhale. Exhale. Center. Inhale. Exhale. This is you meditating.

You can also mindfully sound the ancient, sacred tone, OM, as you exhale. Sounding OM again and again is its own gift of meditation. Here, too... the key is... truly give yourself to sounding the OM. Don't just toss it around off the top of your head. Be *in* it. Again, using ear plugs can enhance your experience. Double enhance. Ear plugs certainly lessen the distracting sounds of the world around you. Also... here comes the "double" part: Ear plugs deepen your focus... magnifying the sound, the vibration as the OM moves thru you. A true ally... helping you be more *in* your OM experience.

Earlier in this chapter, you read… "Release yourself from fussing at yourself." ***That***… just that… is A Huge Gift only you can give to your own well-being. Simply let self-fuss go. (Ha… there's that word "simply" again.)

Instead of harsh and exasperated… imagine your inner dialogue conversing with you in a kind, self-compassionate tone. Just like you are talking to a cherished friend. How would Life be if you didn't fuss, moan, and whine at your self? Imagine the reality of living your Life with no more self-fussing. No moaning. No whining. Sounds cool to me.

Do you hear the tone of voice you use when you are talking to yourself? Do you sound harsh… brusk… exasperated? With perhaps a tad of self-loathing? "You're so messed up." Truth be told… if you talked to your friends the way you talk to yourself… you wouldn't have any friends.

Why so harsh with self… you might ask?

I sure had that irritated, harsh, self-exasperated inner tone going on. Oh yeah… I could really fuss at myself. According to me… I couldn't do anything right. This self-harshness replicates itself. And it sprays. When you're hard on yourself… you are hard on the other people in your Life, too. It's like you can't help it. Immersed in your own painful non-self-acceptance… it's as if you don't know any other way of interacting. Accepting yourself… as you are…

opens doors of awareness and gentle insight. These doors inside you, you did not even know were there to open.

As you are tolerant and forgiving with yourself... you are more tolerant and forgiving of others. This gift of self-acceptance transforms your inner Life. Then radiates out. You are more accepting of other people and the way they are.

Years ago, I sat meditating one day, pouring kindness from the center of my heart out to people I cared about... my kids... Scott... various friends. All of a sudden... unbidden by me... this outpouring stream of kindness turned and came flooding back into my heart! What?! Such a jolt! I physically jerked as I sat there. Pouring kindness to *myself?!*

This had certainly never occurred to me before.

What a concept! Is that allowed? Are there rules? I sat there... stunned. I gently practiced pouring kindness to myself. Is it okay to do this? (Answer: yes.) And then the tricky part. Receiving it. Letting self-kindness in. That took some exercise. It did not come naturally. Are you sure it's okay to do this? Gingerly... I worked it.

As time went on... I worked it like a dog with a bone.

I have learned a lot since that unexpected kindness boomerang moment. Truly The Gift that keeps on giving. Self-kindness is a miraculous healing balm. Transforming. Lifting your awareness.

The way we humans are wired... without consciously applied doses of self-kindness and self-compassion... our journey to greater awareness... our ongoing exploration of self-accountability... succumbs to harsh judgment and self-abuse.

Engaging this awesome, clarifying power of self-kindness... releases you from your own inner neglect and disrespect. Self-abuse is not the ally it pretends to be. Imagine relating to yourself without over-moralizing... without harshness. You release yourself from self-imposed pain... shame... inner conflict.

Our struggle... as human beings... is to rescue ourselves from our own self-condemnation. To redeem ourselves from self-hatred. The realization of this truth... about your human struggle and your own rescue... is cultivated by being kind to yourself.

Becoming more aware of your self-limiting beliefs and habit patterns... you continue to unfetter yourself. You realize you *can* let this stuff go. You can.

These doubts and self-limiting notions... convincing as they may be... are merely habit-thought.

Choosing to be compassionate within yourself... speaking to yourself with kindness... you begin to develop a simple and direct relationship with the way you are. You begin to accept yourself. The way you are. You begin to see you're not "that bad." As you are compassionate with yourself... you are also able to see and accept the other people in your Life... the way they are.

Here is something I want to share with you. Several years ago, I came across the following piece online. It is credited to "Author Unknown." Many times, I've tried to find out who wrote this. Whoever you are... Thank you. I am touched by this clarity and insight.

I am your constant companion.
I am your greatest helper, or your heaviest burden.
I will push you onward, or drag you down to failure.
I am completely at your command.
Half of the things you do,
you might as well turn over to me,
and I will do them ~ quickly and correctly.
I am easily managed ~ you must be firm with me.
Show me exactly how you want something done
and after a few lessons, I will do it automatically.
I am the servant of great people,
and, alas, of all failures as well.
Those who are great, I have made great.
Those who are failures, I have made failures.
I am not a machine,
tho I work I work with the precision of a machine,
plus the intelligence of a person.

You may run me for profit, or you may run me for ruin
~ it makes no difference to me.
Take me, train me, be firm with me,
and I will place the world at your feet.
Be easy with me, and I will destroy you.
Who am I?
I am habit.

"Train me"... decide what you want and how you want your Life to be. "Be firm with me"... get over your resistance... "and I will place the world at your feet." "Be easy with me"... continue to let self-limitation rule... "and I will destroy you."

Establishing your meditation practice is building a habit.
Releasing yourself from negative self-talk
is releasing yourself from a habit.
Teaching yourself to respond rather than react
is exercising a new habit.
Unconscious habit keeps us fettered...
constricted by our self-imposed limitations.
As we build new habits of self-care and well-being
we are strengthening our ability
to become who we are meant to be.
Who we really are.

Fluency

Your regular practice of meditation will give you so much more than you can possibly imagine.

Meditation cools the brain. Which leads us to one of the finest gifts of meditating regularly... the much-needed opportunity to give yourself some space in your inner world. Space between your chaotic thoughts. Space to be more compassionate with yourself... and more compassionate with others. Space for you to embrace and develop awakening awareness within the context of your Life.

The important thing is to *practice* meditating.

Meditate. Don't just think about meditating.

Don't just think about how you "should" meditate... or how you "can't." Reading books or going to lectures about meditation is okay. But do not confuse that with actually meditating. Meditation and thinking are 2 very different things. They happen in 2 completely different parts of you.

As I was studying The Nature of The Soul... my dad began regularly listening to a radio program about meditation. This program did not include actually meditating. He and I would talk about meditation. My dad was a great teacher for me about the difference between reading and talking about meditation... and actually meditating. There is a difference.

Your thinking always wants to win. "Think about ME!" "Have you really thought about this?" "Think some more!" Tis the nature of thinking... to believe every little thinko-babble is soooo important. Really? Here's something your chattering thinkery would never want you to know... in the growth and evolution of human awareness... Intellect is not the final gate.

Meditation is not what you think.

CHAPTER 4

HumanNess 101

"Whoa, Baby... prepare to be astonished!"

Welcome back. I'm sure you enjoyed cruising around in your simulator's Multi-Sensory Apparatus. A good practice excursion. It's an amazing vehicle, isn't it? Such mobility. With its wide variety of sensory input and options.

And how about that food court? Did you try the warm cornbread hush puppies with jalapeno jelly? Oh my gosh! Almost worth going into incarnation for! Oh, and what about the assorted melon platter? Did you have some? I don't know if there's anything more succulent than a selection of ripe melon cubes. Mouthwatering. Oh, that's the term used when you end up with a lot of saliva in your mouth at the thought of something delicious. Saliva just starts squirting in joyful anticipation.

Thank you for returning to your places as our Orientation for Incarnation Prep continues. You may sit, if you'd like, or stand. Position your physical body simulator any way that is comfortable. I'm sure you've found the *swooshing*, thumping body clamor has faded into the background. You hardly even notice it, right? I see you are each moving freely... feeling pretty familiar... at ease with the physical capabilities of your instrument.

If you think these physical characteristics are engaging... Hang On! We are now going to delve into the even trickier... and way fascinating... nuances of your Bio Energy Incarnate Navigation Gear:

1. The psychology of your feelings
2. The pandemonium of your thoughts
3. The lucid purpose of your karma-dharma inheritance

I know. You're thinking, "She's talking about the Emotional Body, right? What *is* the big deal about human emotions? Everyone knows the true function of the Emotional Nature is to be a clear, light-reflective surface for the Light of The Soul. Right? What else is there? Really, how hard can this be?"

Whoa, Baby... prepare to be astonished!

Here at HumanNess 101, we further our exploration of the myriad fascinating aspects of your B.E.I.N.G. Today's excursion will have you wandering thru the veils and filters of the Human Emotional Nature... soon to be your "feelings." As you get born... your human suit comes already enveloped in Your Etheric Sconce... the energy sheath stitched from the fabric of past incarnate traumas and realizations. Nowhere will these traumas and realizations be more vivid than in the scope of your far-ranging Emotional Nature.

As we proceed thru our Orientation Moment, you may notice that certain items of information are stated more than once. In some cases, you may hear similar insights mentioned a number of different times. This is called *repetition*. The human instrument is geared to learn thru repetition. With the first mention of a concept or an idea, a mental seed is planted. Repeating this concept several times waters and fortifies the idea, allowing it to eventually anchor and develop within human understanding. Even tho the B.E. Suit you are currently wearing is a simulant, its functions and needs are purposely near identical to the apparatus of your upcoming incarnate B.E.I.N.G. Thus, we will be utilizing repetition to anchor comprehension. You will find this to be especially true as we discuss and elaborate upon the panoramic scope and mishaps of the human emotional nature.

The truth is... this simulator B.E. Suit you're fitted with here in The Interpretorium can barely accommodate the broad spectrum of the Human Emotional Nature. Along with its own alluring filters and captivating veils... your Emotional Self comes equipt with crazy-high peaks and disturbingly low valleys... thru which most humans blindly stagger about.

You will incarnate with your own assortment of... talents... abilities... foibles... and fascinations. Your incarnate instrument may come with a fear of water... based on past drowning trauma. Or you might find a knowing familiarity draws you to a particular sport or to play a certain musical instrument. You may incarnate with a fascination for fast cars and racing... or conversely... wonder what all that fuss is about. There will be certain hobbies, pursuits, and inclinations that either attract or repel you.

Until you develop a degree of personal awareness and response-ability within your Emotional Nature... as a human incarnate... you will be terrorized by your own anxieties and insecurities. Odd as it may sound to you here, now... when you are there, being human... you will be completely at the mercy of your fears. Ah, yes, fear. Fear will have its fiendish grasp... perpetrated upon you by both your karmic nature and your karmic *nurture*. Nature... those attitudes, orientations, and ways of being you are born with.

Nurture... the emotional architecture of your chosen host family... how they express their caring for you... and for themselves. This "nurture" also includes the effects of the interacting framework and belief structures which will be the construct of your formative years. Stunningly... your inborn attitudes and those early interactions and belief structures will define your emotional view of Life... thru-out your entire incarnation.

Rather than HumanNess 101... you will sometimes hear this emoting facet of incarnate Life referred to as Human-*Mess* 101... which does, yes, it's true, have an unmistakable ring to it. Such crazy business human emotional Life is! There is almost *too* much wide-ranging permutation and restructuring of priorities!

It isn't just a case of "Here I am in my pristine, no-muss, no-fuss emotional body... and I am popping in for a quick and easy human incarnation." You don't just "pop in." Obscure astral veils and many karmic operating factors are activated. As each unit prepares to incarnate... layer upon layer of both inner discourse and outer considerations are called into play.

This procedure begins with the processing of previous incarnate experience and its resulting insight. After all... it is for this "resulting insight" that we go into incarnation. Right? A distillation of each Life's accumulated realizations is presented to The Lords of Accommodation to sculpt future incarnant upgrades and prospects. These fibres of realization are then woven into Your Etheric Sconce.

You will receive from Safe Deposit the etheric web you have been assembling for many incarnations. Your web comes charged with the system structures of your previous incarnate attitudes and awarenesses. This includes your various Life-purpose dharmas... as well as your accumulated strengths and phobias. It is upon this web that your upcoming human instrument will be assembled.

You do not move thru your upcoming human Life as a free agent. This harvest gleaned from past Life perceptions... will shape and influence your inner beliefs... your human interpretive capabilities... and your outer expression.

You are a member of this particular Incarnation Prep Cluster as a result of your past experiences and choices as a human incarnate. Thru those choices... you have developed Your Etheric Sconce to such a fine degree that it innately allows more conscious awareness to express thru you... and thus generate out into Human Life. We thank you for that.

On Planet Earth, inner peace is at a premium. I am going to be completely frank with you. Before you even get born... the fabric of Your Etheric Sconce... and your journey thru the minefield of superimposed determinant factors... will have shaped and molded your emotional self and your mental instrument... into a nearly unrecognizable unit of *self-contempt*. I mean it. As most humans do... you will be disrespecting your own fine self. Crazy, huh? And yet, why in the world would I be telling you this if it wasn't true?

There are externals on Planet Earth over which you will have little or no control. Take, for example, your family of origin. Yes, you are encouraged to state preferences... but that does not mean you always get to be with the people you prefer. The Emotional Life of your human instrument comes karmically pre-connected to certain specific humans. Of most immediate significance will be your biological hosts... your parents... as well as your siblings and other family members. As you continue to move thru your incarnation, you will be repelled by or drawn to... certain school chums... coworkers... and random cohorts.

You arrive on Planet Earth entirely unique. Each person has their own inner life... their own ways of thinking and feeling. Their own interpretations and expression. This personal uniqueness is so distinct that even people who grow up in the same family unit can have completely different views on things, like... the people their parents are... what Life is about... how to navigate in the world... and who's on first.

You will incarnate into a certain locale and a particular time in human history. Again, I know you have been asked to state preferences. I wish I could tell you that you'll get your first choice of locale... but this is not always the case. I can tell you that each individual in this particular Prep Cluster will be incarnating in the time span you have chosen... beginning in the latter half of the 20th Century... into and thru-out the 21st Century.

And I know why you've chosen that exact time sequence!

So clever of you to take incarnation in this particular Era! Totally ingenious! Grabbing the thrill of taking form on Planet Earth just as being human is finally entering the realm of Extreme *Consciousness* Sport! Thru past millennia, for the most part... Humankind On Planet Earth has been focused near exclusively on evolving the physical body and its relation to matter… trade and transport… architecture and manufacturing… business and technology. Now we are entering Humankind's long-awaited Epoch of Consciously Evolving *Awareness*.

Good on you for keeping track of this transition so you can be there for it! Huzzah!

I know you are anticipating your participation in this electrifying evolutionary process! Here at Team Interpretorium... our work is to be sure you are well-prepared as Incarnate Individuals. In order to individuate and experience your "self" as an Individual Incarnate Component... your awareness distillation process has already occurred.

This allows a "drop" of your spiritual essence to inhabit and enliven your incarnate B.E.I.N.G. This essence droplet is your electric "spark." The spark which ignites and animates your living, breathing instrument. And your Entire Incarnating Process. While incarnate... this spark of your distilled essence resides at the very core of your Human Vehicle.

A Useful Tip: You may be wondering... as I inhabit my human form... what will help me recall and activate my spiritual essence? Give your conscious attention to it. Just that. Turn your attention to your spiritual essence. The practice of meditation will offer you ways and means to stimulate this connexion. And to exercise your attentive awareness. As you turn your attention to your Spiritual Body... you will find that your inner presence is alive and available to you.

I know, you're thinking, "Duh... well, of course. Why would you think I don't know that?" And yet, "here" is not "there." While you are actually being human... *many* obstacle illusions will seem to stand "in the way" of your natural self-understanding.

A number of these obstructions and seeming disadvantages will come at you from your external Life. At the same time... you can count on the scope of your *inner* reality to randomly generate many other convincing obstacle illusions and self-imposed limitations. It's almost not fair.

As with so many aspects of Life on Planet Earth... you will find realization of your true essence may indeed be simple... but that does not mean it is *easy*.

As you travel your Path... it is this spark of essence within that will guide and cajole you to assert your participation in this Extreme Consciousness Sport. The Path before you is not one of concrete stepping stones. Your Path is alive. Vibrant with guidance, potential, and possibility.

Humankind... having spent untold centuries stumbling along... assembling and evolving the physical... now comes to the exhilaration of actively developing the conscious *awareness* within that human form. The blossoming growth of human awareness brings with it boundless attainment and reward.

Again let me say... *so* clever of you... keeping an eye on this opportunity and managing to be in line to incarnate. Let's face it... *this*... the evolution of conscious awareness... is really what Incarnating Human on Planet Earth is all about!

Remember, tho... as rewarding and heart-exuberant as it can be... human self-awareness is its own complex cognitive activity. You sit here now all calm and centered... happy... even exhilarated... with your upcoming plans. But this is Planet Earth you are headed for... not Euripdiacez or Kanohaloa. It's *Earth*. Don't ever for a moment underestimate the power of your Earthtone human emotional nature... for good and for despair.

Your mission, should you choose to accept it, is to wake up as soon as possible while in human form.

As you are busy being human... the activity of awakening awareness takes place within the soaring heights and dark recesses of your mental-emotional bodies... your psychological self. Fortunately, the past century on Planet Earth has seen considerable development of tools and resources to access this tender inner terrain.

Even holding these favorable developments in consideration... fear and its toxic effect continue to reign supreme in Human Awareness. I know... as illogical and obtuse as that may be. And, yes, the vast majority of incarnate humans continue to be terrorized by their own emotions. It is true that enlightened ones have always been present in human form. But when considering the general population, human beings are just beginning to acquire a bit of self-insight... a degree of understanding into the nuanced workings of their own emotional nature.

"The melting pot" is descriptive jargon tossed around on Planet Earth... a phrase that does aptly describe Life on Earth. In sociological terms... a "melting pot" is a place, a moment in time, where different races and strata of people... with their assorted rhythms, cultures, and flavors... are all mixed together. Planet Earth itself is one hugely mixed-together place. Every possible variation on the theme of human awareness is found on Planet Earth... from the highly enlightened to the completely shrouded. There are instruments of love, compassion, and kindness... mixed right in with minions of vengeance, hypocrisy, and self-righteous hatred. You will find those who are knowing and tolerant... sitting right alongside those who are ignorant and bigoted. People of every possible stripe, type, and human disposition are "melted" into each and every organization, sect, and group. From bright and brilliant to dense and dented.

At The Interpretorium, we are here to kit you out... with content, context and connexion. To smooth your way into... and, hopefully, thru-out... your human experience. Let me just say, while in human form, it is best to keep in mind... Perspective Is Everything. Your inclinations and attitudes determine your view of your self and your world. As you grow into your incarnation... the gift of basic comprehension may guide you to sense the correlation between your human ego and the Sweet Mystery of Life. Merely being open to this understanding will offer you a Life-altering perspective.

I must say, however... as you are ensconced in the human realm... just because you may understand the mechanics of your instrument... along with your times and your milieu... this does not mean you will actually realize the vast *miracle* of all that is transpiring.

It is helpful to keep in perspective the degree to which the 3 bodies of your incarnate instrument are remarkably intertwined and completely interactive. The well-being of your physical body... the biological chemistry of your brain... the quality of your hormones, feelings, and attitudes... will deeply affect every day of your Life. Especially... your ability to actually engage and direct your thoughts. This will have a major impact on... your emotional nature... your vehicle's general health... and your ability to recollect and accomplish your Clear Light Incarnate Objectives.

As the spark of Soul Light peers forth from your center... it may seem that your mental instrument and your emotional nature participate as co-captains of the team. Your physical body is on board as the brawn... the external expressive. The mental instrument will talk all kinds of fancy... doing every kind of jive to convince you that it is The Captain of the team. Yeah, right. Your mental body so wishes that were true. But hey... don't fall for that. Not even for a minute.

In truth, your wily, wide-ranging emotional nature is the one holding the cards... and wearing the Captain's hat. Twirling the baton and leading the charge. Your emotions are capable of lifting you up or crashing you down. Your emotional self presides over all that happens... and all that doesn't... whether you are consciously with the program... or not.

As much as your thinkery would like you to think otherwise... your thoughts and your crafty emotional wilyness are 2 very different things. Emotions seep in and have their effect... even as thoughts think they are completely in control. Ha!

Earlier in our Orientation Program, I administered simulated physical experience in your B.E. Suit. In today's Program... you will have the opportunity to acclimate to the motion of your human emotion commotion. Fortunately... we have the use of Realizmotron... our state-of-the-art Authentic Scenario Generator. Realizmotron is a stunningly multi-functional device and can be used in an assortment of intriguing modalities. As we continue your Preparation Sequences for Human Life on Earth... this Scenario Generator will allow you to engage in a variety of realistic emoto dioramas.

Let's begin. I will direct and adjust your emotional experience with my handy Realizmo whiz-knobs. Initially, the intensity of these emotional interactions may cause you to feel nauseated... an ill-at-ease feeling in the pit of your stomach. This area is also known as your gut… located in the center of your B.E. Suit. Sometimes emotional reactions are so strong, a person will say, "I feel like I've been kicked in the gut."

As the enormity of your vast and wide emotional nature bursts into focus... take a moment to draw several deep, centering breaths. When you're not feeling too queasy... take a quick peek. An emotional sip. Just a little bit at a time. Allow yourself to survey the temperamental disarray within. Feel the emotive clash. Not too much, at first. Really. Just little sips. It's a humdinger. Draw a breath. Okay. Prepare to be astonished. Zow-Whee! As your emotions come into play... there is definitely commotion! You are *all over* the place!

I'm dialing it back a bit. Remember... keep breathing. Deeply. Slowly. These deep breaths will help ease the quease until you've got your hip-waders on. Ha ha... a little metaphor there. I'm pretty sure I don't even need to explain.

Here's a useful exercise: As you touch in to this realm of your emotional self... experiment with holding on... and then letting go. Engage and hold on to the emotive tumult. You are swept along. What a *spin*! Now, let it go. Release the chaos. Drop it. You are calm and peaceful.

Now again... completely engaged. Pandemonium. Breathe. Now... unattached. Calm. Practice being in your emotional tumult and then... choose to release yourself from it. Choose to release it from yourself. *This* is an inner ability well-worth exercising. Practice a bit more. Deeply in it. Breathe. And release it all. You are being in this world... but not *of* it. Breathe.

Breathe.

What a show, eh?

The human emotional nature is a sight to behold. Could you have even imagined? While we begin with giving you just a taste... to somewhat prepare you... the only way to experience the erratic emo array is to jump in with both feet. This *is* the Human Emotional Excitation that will be yours to maneuver and navigate.

By manipulating the whiz-knobs of Realizmotron's Master Control Panel... I will adjust and modify the EmoNature in your BE Suit. This will allow you an experience of... okay... perhaps more accurately... I will drop-kick you right into this reactive context. Right into actual emotional circumstances... the total emoto hullabaloo you will soon find yourself completely immersed in.

If you were wearing a crash helmet right now... I would say... Hang On To Your Hat!

Okay, so here's what could be called "the funny part"... as capricious and chaotic as this runaway ride is... this emotional pandemonium is *exactly* what draws us to incarnate human. Really. I mean it.

This chaos... this racing adrenaline intensity... this crazy *juice*... entices many. Wily whiz-bang as human emotions are... this is, in fact, one of the Prime Attraction features drawing us to incarnate on this astounding

Planet of Paradox. I'm not making this up. When out of incarnation... the crazed, painful memories fade. In recall, we imagine flailing around in the emotive nature as... "Pure exhilaration! *Tres amusant!* What could *be* more fun?!"

Yet, here is something worth noting... when you are actually on-site... being human... these spinning "attractions"... the soaring, lurching emotions... the difficulties and frustrations... the highs, the lows... the chaos, the pain... make you think, near constantly... "I don't want to *be* here!" The vast majority of humans think, "I don't belong here." "This is too hard!" "It's not worth this much effort." "For what?" Or a newer, very popular euphemism... "This sucks!"

As you are actually in human form... you will hardly ever recall the enthusiasm that drew you to incarnate on Planet Earth. You will be enmeshed in the topsy-turvy crazies that your simulator is experiencing right now. You will identify *as* your emotions. Really. It's true. Bonkers.

In the stew of it all... rarely will you recollect your long-range plan... to transcend the entanglements of human endeavor... to be happy and purposeful as you serve and uplift your fellow humans. Such "best laid plans" get frayed... mislaid... disoriented. Confiscated by the whoop-di-doo.

Yet, it is exactly The Immense Possibility... the Extreme Consciousness Sport... available in the depths of human tumult and turmoil... that draws awareness to incarnate.

This does give one pause.

Residing in spacious cognizance, as you currently do here in The Interpretorium... it is impossible for you to even imagine how completely absorbed you are about to become. Absorbed... in what, right now, seems of absolutely no interest nor consequence. Human, you will be entirely engrossed in the details of your day-to-day mechanizations. "What should I wear?" "My shoes aren't the right color." "Does this make me look fat?" "Where's the beef?" "Are my teeth yellow?" "Should I eat more vegetables?" "Did I win?" "What did he say?" "Was that an insult?" "Should I be upset?" "Is this all there is?" These are the concerns that will keep you totally captivated within the minutiae of self-absorbed trivia.

I hear you scoff. I am absolutely serious.

Much of the ongoing interaction between your mental and your emotional components will involve interpreting emotional circumstances and crafting your response to them. The human thinking/feeling mechanism is most frequently engaged in evaluating external stimulus. "What did he mean by that?" "Is that dog going to bite?" "Did she just come on to me?" The human perceptive mechanics are all about... ongoing evaluating of input... and devising output. A reaction. Appropriate, or otherwise.

Of course, we all want to incarnate as conscious and aware as possible. Of course we do. However, I do have to tell you... as you contemplate your upcoming incarnation... be aware that just because something makes sense to you here... this does not in any way guarantee it will make sense to you there. It turns out, when you are human on Planet Earth... Awakening is an *option*.

Recalling your past incarnate experience may have you feeling familiar with certain features of your human equipment. There is no assurance that awareness... that familiarity... will be readily available to you in your upcoming human Life. The possibility does exist that you may have an insightful grasp of certain aspects of your human paraphernalia from the get-go. Some... a few... are born that way. The majority are not.

Most likely, awakening will come on the fly. With or without spiritual practices... you will fight your way thru the dross... drawn, somehow, to developing your awareness. Remembering Your True Self. Finding a way. As time and busyness play out. Or, perchance, not at all.

Yes... it is possible to live an entire human incarnation with not one awakening glimpse of the Vast Dimensionality of Life. That Life which lives within and beyond all things. Some would consider such an oblivious incarnation unskilled... a waste, even. A failure. Harsh, yes. Understandable, yes. Whether you are in incarnation or out... it is a sadness to observe a human Life wasted. In ignorance.

Foolish addictions. Rage and vengeance. Misguided desires. Truth is... you do "learn" from residing in an unawakened Life. I say "residing" because it can't really be called "living." One would hope... what you learn... is the uselessness of opportunity squandered. And not to do it that way again.

Now, there are times you may go into incarnation to accompany a friend or associate. You choose to be in human form... based on a karmic agreement... to assist or enable that other person to evolve in some way. You incarnate more for them than for yourself. Hazy as you may be to the calling of your own Path... this can lead to living your whole Life dulled and unaware. Even incarnating as a consort... there are choices to be made. The choice that always serves you best is to wake up within your human Life. Remember... you came into human form to be more than a sidekick. Remember what you are there for. It is always a good idea to get the most awareness bang for your incarnation buck.

Looking around... as we are all here in the "bodies" of our Bio Energy simulants... you see that the unique physical characteristics of every human unit allows each to be singularly recognized. Well... each person's emotional nature is... if anything... even *more* nuanced and specific. You will enter this incarnation ensconced in the emotional reactive nature you are born with... shaped by past-life influences... and distinct astral qualities. Some people are born cranky... destined to become cranky, irritable, and irritating children. Their irritation is reflected back to them by the adults in their environment. Crankiness and turmoil prevail. Others are born with a sublime disposition. By nature... they interact with Life and those around them in a gentle, pleasant way. As a result... their world out-pictures these charmed qualities. Interestingly... the neurological chemicals in the brain play a major role in the way a person interacts with their Life. Brain chemicals. You could say, individuals are bio-chemically set-up from the very get-go.

Now, here is something you are going to find fascinating. One way you can see the uniqueness of each human's emotional packaging is by watching several people as they each have a completely different reaction to exactly the same stimuli. Allow me to demonstrate. Could I please have 4 volunteers to help me with this presentation? A volunteer is someone who says, "Sure, I'll play along." Just come and join me up here. Ah, thank you.

Here we have 2 estro-infused components and 2 testo-laden units. For identification purposes, I will give you names... the personal designator used by each human. You 2 estro units will be called Marcy and Ashley. Our 2 testo units will be Jeff and Greg. Now I will employ the Realizmo Scenario Generator to create a visual diorama for us here. Each of our volunteers will be encoded with their own emotional reaction to our sensory set-up. Thanks to Realizmotron being the multi-functional gizmo it is... each of you observing will be able to experience the emotions our 4 volunteers are feeling.

Now... volunteers... please exit stage left.

Observers, you can see the visual scene Realizmotron is generating... a lush, green forest on a sunny day. Hear the birds singing in the trees? And you can smell the fragrances of moss and greenery. Do you see the earthen path winding thru the forest? A lovely "great outdoors" serenity permeates the scene. I'm lovin' this.

Now, will our 4 volunteers please enter... walking along this path... chatting with one another... enjoying the lush green scenery as you stroll along. It's such a beautiful day. La la la...

Wait! Look out! A big snake! Darting out from the underbrush! Slithering across your path!

"*Shriek!*" Marcy stops dead in her tracks. Immediately feeling menaced... she is experiencing genuine fear. Did you feel her startle? And now her fright? Yet, Marcy is holding her own. She finds... as long as nothing scarier happens... she is willing to be slightly intrigued.

Ashley bends down to get a better look at this fascinating creature. "Wow! I've always wanted to see a sunbeam snake up close! Look at the play of light on its iridescent scales as it undulates. What a beaut!" Do you feel Ashley's enthusiasm? And how engaged she is?

Greg? Where'd Greg go? He is nowhere to be found. Terrified, he has bounded back up the path and out of sight. Gone. "Greg?"

Jeff could not be less interested. A snake... so what? He's gazing around at the greenery. "I wonder what's for lunch?"

One stimulus. Four completely different reactions.

The force of each person's reaction comes from the entirety of their... karmic... ingrained... multi-experienced... self. Ashley's fascination or Greg's terror have very little to do with the snake. The snake is just the snake... its usual, slithery serpent self. Doing what snakes do.

Now, get this... not only does each human come equipt with their own individual reaction(s)... each person will experience and remember and retell the story in their own diverse way.

Thank you volunteers. You may return to your places. As we power down Realizmo, has anybody seen Greg? Jeff, would you please look out in the hall for him? Thanks.

Okay. Continuing our investigation into the peculiarities of the Human Emotional Nature... this must include exploration of the enigmatic fluctuations rippling thru-out the emotional *environment* you are about to enter. It's quite unlike here. A major contrast to this realm of pure cognitive reality we're in now. Way different.

When you are actually on Planet Earth... let me see... how best to say this? The emotional environment on Planet Earth is vast... and somewhat askew. This realm is awash in provocative astral structures and perplexing emoto architecture. These agitating constructs are flooded with Swirling Emotional Forces you presently would not even know how to contemplate. Residing in... the veils... the miasma... that envelop Planet Earth... these emotive forces are not to be foreseen. Nor can they be foretold.

These Swirling Emotional Forces are causal agents yearning to express. They live to act out... to exhibit... to manifest... within the Emotional World on Planet Earth. Here's the kicker... you're going to love this... the only way these zealous emotional forces can demonstrate is thru a human host-expressive. To "act out"... these Emo Forces need a human to "act out" thru. This means unsuspecting, incarnate you!

These Emotional Forces ignite and fan their operations under the radar of human awareness. The struggle and conflict humans are obsessed within are the result of the exertion of these elemental forces. As all elementals are, these forces are fierce... single-minded... tenacious. And, until the incarnate human attains an effective degree of conscious awareness... these elemental forces Must Be Obeyed. They're like an emotional freight train roaring down the track. And you get flattened. Smooshed. You are the minion of these forces before you even know what hit you.

Unconsciously... humans allow themselves to be the instrument... the expression of... rage... uncertainty... malaise... anxiety. Grouchiness. This "allowing" happens without a whiff of conscious consideration. You will be completely unaware that you are, indeed... a human action figure for the interplay of these swirling, emoting powers. Vengeance. Retaliation. Misery. There you are... at the mercy of what you perceive to be "your" emotional reactions. You will believe the unruly antics of these elemental forces *are* you!

Unconscious, unaware humans are convinced, "I *am* my emotions." "I have no choice but to react the way I always have." "This is just the way I am." "This is how I do me."

Encumbered in human awareness, you will be completely unaware of these Swirling Emotional Forces. This is an adorable thing about the human ego fixation. Humans believe they are *"IT"*... the end-all, be-all on Planet Earth. Humans think they're so "on top of it"... *so* smart... so "top of the food chain." They reside blissfully unaware of The Larger Planetary Shenanigans being played out on this blue-green orb. Humans think it's all about them. The Best and The Brightest! Dominion. Intellect. Self-absorbed.

Bacteria and viruses have been playing their Wily Game on this planet since time and beyond. Taking plants and humans out left and right... decimating populations. Unseen. Unconfronted. It is in these last few centuries humans have even become aware that bacteria exist. Viruses revealed themselves to humans less than 150 years ago. Only in the past 100 years, or so, have humans begun to confront them... sometimes successfully. Sometimes not. Bacteria and viruses have still more cunning Games to play. Can anyone say, "Antibiotic-resistant?"

Then there are also the ever-provocative ups and downs of the Carousel of Estrogen and Testosterone. Riotous goings-on. Sure, humans are aware of "female" and "male"... the ensuant attractions... the pleasure and discontent of sexual activity. They simply have no idea of the broader scope this excitation of hormones plays. It's a doozy! And it keeps humans compelled.

Along these same lines... invisible to human awareness... yet stunningly manipulative... are the vast, astral structures... the aforementioned emotional architecture. And those Swirling Emotional Forces. With humans but their unwitting pawns. Like I said, humans are "action figures" to these cunning forces. Marionettes.

As you know... the Higher Spirit Forces' only "means to be"... the only way Greater Awareness can touch the incarnate world... is thru a human host-expressive. Each incarnate human is, in potential... the hands and feet... the speech and actions... of Higher Awareness. Of God.

It turns out this is also true in the domain of these Swirling Emotional Forces. What's the only way these Emotional Forces can show up on Planet Earth? As a human host allows their body to become the expression of anger, doubt, anxiety, malice. This is also true as the forces of compassion, joy, fulfillment, and a giving heart find their human expression. It takes a host-expressive.

I am currently focusing more on the hurting emoto components because... as a human incarnant... your belief in this self-constricting pain will generate near-continual distress and confusion. This jumble of hurting emotion convinces humans their Life is crap. Sadly, the majority of humans see Life itself as... harsh... deceptive... not to be trusted. Feeling dissed by Life gives people permission... to be offensive... aggressive... hostile. Hurting others.

It is thru their oblivious human hosts that these vexing Emotional Forces race about, unchallenged. Coming into play thru groups of host-expressives... these elemental forces feed upon each other. Their influence grows... thrives. They generate increased bedlam... showing-up and acting-out thru assorted humans.

You can see that for the perpetrator, this acting out... this offense and aggression... is short-sighted, indeed. The effects of their uncontrolled, uncaring actions only generate for themselves more grimy karma and long-term repair orders. They'll need more than a biological oil change between incarnations.

Cynicism and despair... harming... anxiety... numbness and apathy... dominate much of human inner Life. Negative... desperate... self-limiting feelings... are not all there is to the Human Experience. But they surely do get the most press... and more than their fair share of human attention.

Sadly, it does not occur to human beings that it is with their own attention... that they, themselves, feed these hurting, painful thoughts and emotions. Focusing on despair and anguish *nourishes* despair and anguish. These emotions thrive. They grow robust.

As you are human... the emotions and thoughts you give your attention to become what is "real" for you.

How do The Swirling Emotional Forces play thru me? This does not enter your mind for even a second. A huge part of your experience on Planet Earth will be created, colored, energized by these Forces... and you will not even realize you are being played.

At this point... remember... relax. Unclench your jaw muscles. Breathe. Unclench again. Don't make this harder on yourself than it needs to be.

Deep breath.

As a tool for understanding this phenomenon... Realizmotron is now pumping a colorized version of the Swirling Emotional Forces into the room. The colors allow you to see these elemental forces move... undulate... and have their way. Incarnate humans do not have a clue that they are auto-loading conduits... continually at the mercy of these propelling Emotional Forces.

Here's how it happens... humans have no idea. As they are triggered in their emotional world... the latch of their emotive unit pops... their emoto hatch flies open... and The Forces dive in. Quicker than quick! These elemental forces do not fool around. They are on it in a heartbeat.

These whirling demonstration colors allow you to see the very moment a Swirling Emotional Force enters its human host. The emoting human is instantly overtaken by anger, sadness, anxiety... or, also visible... and viable... kindness, compassion, joy. You can watch as the colorized emotion shoots thru the emoto hatch and consumes its host's reacting capacity.

Now expressing thru a human vehicle... this Emotional Force is having its moment... its hours, weeks, years. Infecting the emotional environment on Planet Earth. Some ill-guided groups of humans give extended expression to these hurtful forces as they make it a point to infect their young.

These infecting adults provide further expression to these Forces... as they pass along animosity... vengeance... retribution. Contaminating their younglings. Such foolishness. Rather than looking to transform or uplift... these adults train the next generation... teaching them to carry on hating as they do. Grinding on. It goes without saying... this is not evolutionarily productive. The cycles of incarnating humans continue to spew... hating and hurting... until those involved finally come to the realization they are getting absolutely nowhere. They might fool themselves... thinking they are empowered by their hatred and vengeance. In the Greater Scheme of Things, this is not so. Their actions are, in fact, pathetic. Useless. Wasteful.

Remember, this colorization is for demonstration purposes only. Altho, you know... there are times when a person will say they "see red" or "feel blue." Or they might be "green with envy." When you are actually incarnate... the Forces show no colors. Don't we wish they could be seen! Here at Team Interpretorium... we use these representative visuals... to give you a symbolic context... hopefully to help you grasp these elemental emoto issues.

I hear you thinking *you* will be immune. "That ain't gonna happen to me, Sistah. I'm not gonna be no emotional action figure." Yeah, well, let's give this a whirl . . .

Engaging Realizmo, I will also... via my whiz-knobs... be adjusting your emoto sensory filters... the ones that simulate your emotional reactive impulses.

I'm going to divide you all into three groups... here... here... and here. For the center one-third, I am engaging Realizmotron to amp the filter aperture engaging your emotional reactions. We'll start slow. Here's the scenario... you're sitting in your hot car in traffic... for way too long. And you've got places to be! You're feeling frustrated. There! Did the rest of you see the Forces of Frustration rush in? Okay, you've been sitting and sitting. In the hot sun. On the freeway. With exhaust fumes. So annoying. Watch... annoyance zips right in. Your armpits drip with sweat. This so sucks. All of a sudden, some jackass whips out of nowhere and edges his car into your lane. Right in front of you! What? *What?* You are angry! And, justifiably so! Who does this jerk think he is?! He can't just cut you off like that! You are So Mad! Observers who are not emotionally engaged... did you see the Force of Anger surge right in? Hot and mad!

Now this one-third of you over here... I am amplifying your emo sensitivity fibres. You can feel this spraying anger. In reaction to it... you are starting to feel anxious. Did you feel your emoto hatch open? Probably not. But now, anxiety is gushing thru-out you. It feels like it *is* you. "I hate being around people who are so mad. It makes me feel queasy. Really uncomfortable." "Did I do something to make them mad?" Instantly... hormones in the physical body are engaged and begin to squirt... the heart beats faster... capillaries contract... the mouth is dry... little beads of sweat break out on your brow. And you are feeling... well... anxious. Unsettled. Disturbed.

The group of observers over here in this 3rd group, who are not currently broiling mad... see how the Force of Anxiety immediately takes advantage of the reflexive situation and zips into the emoto instrument? The troubled uneasiness of anxiety overtakes its host and begins to oscillate out into the world.

Okay... this remaining one-third of you... I am engaging your compassion musculature. You feel a deep understanding flood in. You find you are not hooked by the first group's anger... the anger that made the second group uneasy and agitated. You are now feeling compassion for them both. Did you feel the swirling force of compassion stream into your instrument? You find it completely understandable that being stuck in traffic and getting cut off would cause anger and upset. Compassionately... you empathize with the angry reaction.

From your perspective... it's easy to see how those raging emotions only make a difficult situation worse.

As you observe the anxious group... you totally comprehend their agitation. It's scary to be in the presence of another person who is raging and angry. There you are compassionate... observing the emotional business of the other 2 groups. You feel a gentle concern. You're just not caught up in the hoopla.

Now I am adjusting everyone's emotional nature to a balanced, centered level. I know those of you who experienced compassion are feeling at peace. We're going to take a few moments to give those in the angry group some space to cool down... and give the anxious ones a chance to regain composure.

I'm sure you are finding that being manipulated by emotion leaves you feeling jerked around. Drained.

Drawing a few deep, centering breaths can be very helpful. Increased oxygen calms the physical body... soothes the adrenaline response... brings a degree of balance back to your emotions.

What's that, you say? It's not fair that you and your group got all hot, bothered, and rage-full... while the folks in this group were all cool, calm, and contemplative? Here we have a perfect example of the vagaries of human emotion in play. Even here in The Interpretorium, the Forces of "Not fair!" and "Why not them?" dive into the fray. "Why me?!"

Of course, the joke is "Why *not* you?"

Yeah, I know... there are some who find that not-so-funny right now. You will find humans can be quite touchy about their emotions. Sensitive to the point of distraction. Yes, that, too, is a little joke… emotional "distraction" being one of the enduring pitfalls of human awareness.

Note to self: Gentle humor is frequently not well-received in the heat of things. Humans have a substantial sensitivity to feeling "laughed at." Even when you assure them, "I'm laughing *with* you." Doesn't always go over so well.

Well, that was all quite a ride, wasn't it? You have to admit, the astounding thing in this demonstration of the Emotional Forces is that once they get you... They've Got You. When you're in the midst of a human emoto maneuver... you identify as if the emotional reaction *is* you. In the thick of the emotional clinches... you will have very little... if any... conscious awareness that you have a choice as to how you respond or react.

When given an inch... these Swirling Emotional Forces will – whoosh! Grab you! Like that! And take a mile. Five miles. Twenty! If you let them.

In the complex scope and structure of the human emotional spectrum... there are numerous factors continually at work. Karma. Family. Society. Your own inner wiring. Regurgitated reaction to past experience. Fear. Many diverse ingredients make up each person's emotional stew.

Again, I am inclined to mention... as you are human... who you learn to be... and how you learn to be... is strongly influenced by your childhood environment. Particularly, your primary caregiver's reactive nature. This will especially affect your built-in tendency to hang on to slights and misunderstandings. Or to let them go. Also impacted will be your ability... or inability... to forgive and release.

Forgiveness is a powerful tool.

As a human being, when you "can't forgive," you will only be keeping yourself tangled up in the painful conflict. "I'll never forgive my 8th grade teacher for embarrassing me in front of that cute Billy Drew!" Reality check: Your 8th grade teacher doesn't even remember you. You may think, "I'm not ever going to forgive. That'll really show them!" Well, little buddy, it ain't about "them." You're only keeping the ache alive and hurting inside yourself. Let it go. Forgive "them." Forgive yourself.

Forgiveness... or not forgiving... is an excellent example of how the vast majority of incarnate humans twist possibility... and end up victimized by their own emotions. Each person is *fiercely* manipulated by their own perplexing, inner nature. Sadly... humans allow themselves to be ill-used... ill-advised... by this very aspect of being that should be a wondrous ally.

Another salient point to consider... humans want Life to be fair... easy... pleasant. They react hard when it is not. Completely understandable. But, you know, sometimes Life is just not fair... nor easy... nor pleasant. No harm. No foul. Just isn't.

Okay... onward. Here's an emoto mini-fill. Draw in a deep breath and slowly let it out. You will feel a progression of emotional states as I adjust my whiz-knobs. If you can... keep an eye on the colorized Swirling Forces. Doubt and uncertainty are seeping in. Along come their emoto companions... dread and agitation. Uncertainty... dread... now you're feeling vulnerable. Fear swoops in. Vulnerable... shaky... insecure. A flood of anger. Humans do not like feeling fearful... insecure... vulnerable. They leap to anger because they can't deal with feeling their fear. It seems that leap to anger is "easier." Now anger has you. Really angry. Damn angry! Grrrrr! Really? Anger masking your fear is *easier?*

For the one-third of you who, a few minutes ago, had been just sitting here being compassionate... this "damn angry!" is quite a ride, isn't it? And... if allowed... it will just keep on keepin' on.

But now... we will just let the anger go. I am adjusting the whiz-knobs. Draw a deep breath. Exhale... releasing. And another deep breath. Release.

Do yourself a favor and do not for one moment anticipate human emotional Life to be a linear excursion. There you are, feeling all peaceful and loving. The next instant... a jolt of external stimuli. "Johnny, you just spilled fudge sauce on her white carpet!" You are furious. Enraged. Humiliated. Embarrassed. Mad. That clumsy kid!

One minute, you're just fine. Then, triggered or not... swooping under your awareness radar... these Emotional Forces dart in and you're *got*. They can come from out of nowhere. Behind... below... beyond... your conscious awareness. Gotcha!

Your reacting emotions become the show... the whole show. You are not *you* anymore. Who *you* are in the moment... in the situation... the interaction... has officially been grabbed. You *are* outrage. You *are* sadness. You *are* doubt. Insecurity. Misery. Angst.

It's as if you don't get to choose who you're going to be in this time and place. Fear is triggered. You lash out... wanting to hurt. Because you feel hurt... afraid. Your emotional environment... your family or coworkers... the world around you... gets sprayed. Victimized... just as you are. Victimized by your own pain and fear.

Now let's try something else. I am adjusting your emoto flow to prepare you for another experience.

As I mentioned before... the Forces of compassion... of joy, fulfillment... even insightful humor... are also ready to pour in. Here's an emo squirt of humor and joy. Ahhhh... ha ha! You just want to laugh out loud. Go ahead, give a chuckle. Savor the sweet goodness. Delight in it. Let it juice you. Sweeeet.

Here's a potent exercise... allow this joy and delight to thrill you! To fill you! Just as much as your rage twanged you. Fortify your joy. Let it be big inside you. Strong. Real.

Many times, humans "believe in" their anger... much more than they "believe in" their happy. Like their anger is all serious and "real," while their happy is ephemeral... a lightweight. Truth is, based upon observation... we have conclusive evidence... anger and grumpiness don't always have to win.

There are adult humans who pass their years in grudgement... grouchy... crabby... in a fuss. Once grumped... grumpy people believe in and hold onto their grump. Like they don't know no better. They want to share their special grump. They want you to believe how important their grump is. Sometimes, it's hard not to grump right back at them. There's really no good reason for you to participate in their grump. That is not a requirement. When they toss their grump ball at you... you *can* just put it down and walk away. Let them have their grump. They can be grouchy all they want. You have better things to do.

Then of course... there are the hot-headed. Some humans seem to be perpetually steamed. Testy. Short-fused. Like it doesn't occur to them they could be living their Life any other way. Spewing in your direction... they either want to blame you for their irrationalities... or they want you to be all fired up with them. Again, it is not a requirement that you accept their blame. Nor act like them. Sometimes... you just flare back. It can be hard to resist their big fuss. You want to hot mess back at them. But here's what it really comes down to... hot-headed is only "attractive" or considered "useful" to the hot-headed ones. You do not *have to* combust along with them.

Please keep this in mind... in the human realm... joy and fulfillment have as much to teach you as pain and limitation do. Maybe even more.

For some people... choosing joy and happiness seems a foreign concept. Joy? Happy? Huh? It really is a choice. Exercise your joy. Give it some fresh air. Take your joy out for a walk now and again. In a moment of random abandon... *choose* to feel joyful... happy... glad. Embrace it. Exercise it. Share it with others.

Even if you can only sustain joy and happiness for a moment... that counts! You build your tolerances for gladness as you give it your attention. Give it some more. Allow. Stretch. Exercising your joy and compassion muscles brings you unanticipated insight... understanding... reward. Relish a deep sense of gratitude. Keep working it. As you live in loving kindness inside yourself... you foster in your Life... expressions of encouragement. You actively value those around you.

Now, I have for you a shower of active valuing... 2-fold. Here you will feel the experience... the grace... of feeling valued yourself. Quite rewarding. Wow... I'm valued. A joy to your heart. Now... you will be filled with the experience of valuing others. In your upcoming incarnation... you'll *especially* want to exercise this with the children your Life touches. Let children know how much you like them... how much you *see* them. A young human thrives and flourishes as they feel loved and valued. Let children know your Life is better... richer... because they are a part of it. Because it will be.

When it comes to feeling valued... as it turns out... *you* will have to be the one who starts that cycle as you begin to value yourself. A totally worthwhile exercise. As your awareness grows thru-out your incarnation... this will become increasingly clear... more than anything, people want to feel valued. Seen. Respected. For the contribution they are making to the world around them. Make it a practice to value others. Make it a practice to value yourself.

When you are human... waking up in your Life is completely optional. Some humans... when entertaining the possibility of "waking up"... think, "Ugh!" "So much work." "Too hard." "Boring." "Not for me." "I don't even know what that means!"

Others hear the concept of "waking up" and think, "At last!" "This is exactly what I've been looking for!" "I'm all over it!" "Thank Goodness."

Believe me... your awakening process does not call for "too much." It is neither arduous nor a strain. Waking up only calls you to be aware... responsive... engaged. Waking up guides you. To value your Life. To see the affirming contributions you are making. To see the affirming contributions others are making. Waking up guides you to participate in your Life in a different way. In a constructive, uplifting way. In an encouraging way.

I know all of you sitting here are thinking, "Why wouldn't everybody *want to* wake up? Isn't waking up while in human form exactly what we go to Planet Earth to do?! To be awake and aware while *in* human form?" Well, yes. Yes, it is. However, please keep in mind... as I've pointed out... as you head into incarnation... there are astral veils and convoluted emotional architecture conspiring to cloud your vision. To dull your knowing. To keep you unaware of your true incarnate purpose.

Have I mentioned… for a good while during your incarnation, it will not even occur to you that there is waking up to do? Yes, I'm sure I've mentioned that.

Many incarnate humans have leaks around their emoto hatch where pain, doubt, and fear continually dribble in. These 3 "dribbles" are the prime generators convincing human beings that they are unworthy. The near constant yammering of… doubt… fear… pain… builds a habit of unworthiness within their human host. This habit of unworthiness… of not feeling valued… convinced that "something's wrong with me"… keeps human beings imprisoned in the asylum of "my Life sucks and it's always going to be this bad." Turns out, this is not true. But it sure seems true. Your human self is believing… "I'm always going to be this miserable."

Here's a clue: Things change. When you are human… steeped in personal misery… make the time to reach out and help another person. Move beyond stewing about yourself. Give time and attention to lift up someone else. Things change.

I'd like to offer you a useful tidbit to keep in mind about your process of waking up while human. As a degree of awakening is attained… the human incarnant begins to sense… and then see… where the leaks are in their emotional mechanism. These leaks allow the Swirling Emotional

Forces to have their way... running willy-nilly thru Human Life. The leaks can be repaired, as you find where they are.

You do not have to continue being "played"... victimized by emotional poop. You come to realize... "It's not a requirement that I always act the part of the oblivious puppet."

Becoming more aware... you learn to "repurpose" the emotional hoopla. By your choice and intention, the energy of these elemental forces *can* be redirected. They can be oriented toward more manageable, enjoyable, and contributing outcomes.

It all boils down to... you *can* choose which Emotional Forces you allow to express thru you. You can choose to be used by compassion and kindness. You can *choose* to be centered and fair-handed in the midst of a difficult situation. You can even choose to shout and emote... sometimes, that's what it takes to get the attention of those you're with. The crucial factor here is that you *know* you are choosing to shout and gyrate. You are not merely an unaware victim of your own emotional tantrum... rude and out-of-control... spraying your anger hither and thither.

As you move thru your human Life... waking up gives you awareness tools... to break the chains that bind you to pessimistic self-belief habits.

Here is a point well-worth remembering: Until you go thru a major change in your own short-sighted consciousness...

you will continue to move thru your Life allowing your past to determine your future.

Using a page from *The Advanced Realization Playbook*... let's continue to unravel the hold these Elemental Emotional Forces have on human awareness.

As you sit here viewing all of these colorized Forces, it looks as if there are myriad emotions swirling about. Let me make a slight adjustment here. You will now observe all of the different colors becoming only 2 colors. Only 2 emotions. Love and Fear.

All of the colors of rage... anxiety... revenge... meanness... become one color... the color of Fear. The "negative," difficult, aggressive emotions all distill to Fear. Now you are seeing the colors of kindness... compassion... understanding... joy... become the color of Love. At their very core, all of the "positive," uplifting, liberating emotions are actually Love.

Love and Fear are the only 2 emotions at play in Human Town. The very circumference of human perception and emotion resides within the Spectrum of Love and Fear.

People who are angry are actually afraid. People who act all pissy are actually afraid. People who are doubting and anxious are afraid. Afraid of what their Life is doing. Afraid of what Life will bring. Afraid of not being perceived as "right." Afraid of doing something "wrong." Afraid of not having "enough." Afraid they will "lose" somehow.

A significant truth about your Life on Planet Earth: In every moment of your human Life, you are either being an instrument of Love or you are being an instrument of Fear.

Building on this awareness... we have another choice morsel from *The Advanced Realization Playbook*. This spectrum of Love and Fear is based within the fundamental misperception dominating human awareness. This flaming misperception is the deeply painful belief that "I am separate from God." I am separate from Source. I am separate from the Great Generating Creative Center of All Life. And just to give this an exceptionally painful twist... I have been *cast out*. Banished. Cut off. Abandoned. I am forsaken... discarded... unworthy. Unloved.

I feel the wave of shock pulsing thru your collective awareness. I know! Believing you are separate from God!? How can that be!?! And, yet... unawake and unaware... this is where humankind lives. A self-generated hell. A fiery delusion. Here we have a case where fear appears to be winning.

Anyone... here in cognizant reality... will tell you this sense of "being separate" cannot be further from The Truth. As if a droplet of water could be separate from the ocean in which it resides. Yet within the realm of human awareness... this misbelieving pervades every particle of being... thought... word... and deed. For many people, their world... inner and outer... is bleak and dark. Life itself is to be feared. They gather evidence to prop up their dismal belief. Be afraid. Be *very* afraid. This fear dominates... giving its texture to all that is seen... believed... lived.

This false belief generates a sense of being separate from others... which allows humans to hurt others as they, themselves, feel hurt. Believing they are separate from the environment... with "dominion" over the plant and animal kingdoms... humans allow themselves to disrespect... disregard and destroy... the very elements of existence which they rely upon to survive. This belief in being separate has a particularly destructive effect on a human's inner Life. Feeling abandoned... forsaken... unloved... creates an inner environment that allows hate, vengeance and emotional desolation to fester.

Speaking of fester... this misaligned sense of separation makes it easy to see the fierce festerment of greed within Human Life. The forces of greed and selfishness have a stranglehold on human imagination and on so many other facets of Life on this blue-green orb. Minions of fear... the forces of greed and selfishness pollute the planet. This toxic pollution occurs emotionally... mentally... and physically. "I gotta get mine! Mine's gotta be the biggest!" Really? You are so missing the point.

Regrettably... blinded by this belief they are forsaken... shackled by their misguided pain... humans fail to see the

Interconnectedness of All Things. On Planet Earth and Beyond.

Imagine if humans "believed" in the Interconnectedness of All Things... multi-dimensional as it is in all its splendor... just as much as they "believe" in their anguish... and that they are "separate from God." Yes... that is worth pause. Take a moment to imagine.

If "the splendor of Life" were *as believed* as "the anguish of Life"... Life on Planet Earth would be transformed.

Transformed.

We'll allow this particular musing to move us in a completely different direction. Altho this does fall in the realm of multi-dimensionality. Let's talk about your Magic Decoder Ring! Well, okay, more accurately... your Awareness Upgrades... Recall Button... and your Enhanced Wiring Package.

In light of your upcoming foray into incarnation... here at HumanNess 101... we have prepared a cadre of tools, clues, and insights to help you to:

1. Move beyond the stupid stuff
2. See the meaning in your day-to-day experiences
3. Grasp the significant insights
4. More readily embody a finer degree of conscious awareness

Your presence in this particular Incarnate Prep Cluster has its own significance. Here in this Cluster... based on your Life choices in incarnations past... you are receiving many perks... along with an assortment of high-quality awareness benefits. The most bodacious asset? You have been selected to incarnate human in The Relatively Awake & Aware Model. That, in and of itself, will be beyond helpful. A real treat! This means your wiring network comes packed with... super-fine sensory skills... enhanced situational awareness... and bonus recall circuits. You will also find your incarnate B.E.I.N.G. spliced with additional multipurpose enhancement features.

I do want to mention that, while you're actually in human form... especially in your younger years... your enhanced sensitivity may prove somewhat problematic. As a child, your parents or others in your Life... adults... peers... may tell you, "Don't be so sensitive." "You think too much." "You're wasting your time trying to nurse that sick animal back to health." You may find this annoying. They can't help themselves. The Forces of being annoyed and being annoying have cut a deep trench in the human psyche.

Along these same lines... there will be things about you that make perfect sense to you... but do not necessarily "make sense" in the context of your family and your early learning environment. You may wonder mightily about this choice you made... being born to your particular parental hosts. As I mentioned earlier... you'll find all types of temperaments stewing together in this "melting pot" on Planet Earth. You may find your close family members to be... as they say... "cut from very different pieces of cloth" than you are. This has the potential, at times, to be quite refreshing. Other times, not so much.

One of the many reasons you are in this particular Prep Cluster... receiving these enhancements... is because, in past human incarnations, you made choices... and did the work... to equip yourself with deep compassion and wide understanding. You wisely utilized this understanding to uplift your fellow humans and make Life on Planet Earth a better place. You have managed in past incarnations to awaken while in human form. Thru the crafting of your own human experience, you have come to understand the significant grace of evolving toward loving kindness. Good on you.

Now, in The Evolving Scheme of All Things... your "reward" is to receive these actively enhanced features as you spiral headlong into the density of human form. Here at Team Interpretorium... in the midst of your colossal undertaking... our ongoing intent is to render your destiny a bit less complicated.

In our Incarnate Prep Cluster here... we focus on implementing your human instrument so you can begin to wake up at a young age. "Young" is, of course, relative. Even 70 years on Planet Earth is "younger" than 80 years. Every tad of awakening counts. Here's something worth grokking... when you begin waking up in your young adult Life... it makes the rest of your incarnant journey much smoother... more purposeful... and definitely a lot more enjoyable.

One of your most useful enhancement tools will be your "Recall + Retain Button." Mainly, you're going to want to "recall and retain" why in the world you find yourself on Planet Earth in the first place. Fraught with confusion, doubt, and anxiety... some variation on "What am I doing here?!"... is the major FAQ. The most frequently asked question... indeed.

While in human form... you'll especially want to recall your loving intent... your purpose... your mission. Your joy. This wide-ranging remembering... blazes in thru your heart... calms twitchy nerves... opens your eyes... and sets your feet upon your Path.

Accessing your Recall + Retain Button, you'll want to retrieve your incarnate assignment. "I am here to..." Your growing awareness will guide you to focus on embodying human qualities that have you showing up... being kind... and contributing to the situation(s) you're in.

Show up. Be kind. Contribute.

You'll especially want to "retain" your purposeful resolve. Remember... as stated previously:

> Your mission, should you choose to accept it,
> is to wake up as soon as possible
> while in human form.

Right now, let's give your Recall Button a spin. Engage this upgrade function. Push that button. As with all of the enhancement features on your Magic Decoder Ring... easy access occurs in the artifact cones of the astral-etheric realm. Which in the human domain means... this all happens in your inner Life. Attaining awakened awareness is an inside job. This is one of the best reasons to develop a strong meditation practice.

We don't refer to the human domain as "density" because we think it sounds cute. Dense is an apt description. Thick. Heavy. Dim. Definitely "non-buoyant." In this density domain... it usually takes a big *whap!* in the personal force field to grab human attention and turn it beyond narrow habit-thought fixations. This *whap!* can come in many forms. It can be the painful end of a relationship... or unexpectedly losing a job... a house... or financial backing. It can even be a difficult realization about your self. There are many variations on being drop-kicked into a dark, hurting place inside. So dark that all you can subconsciously consider doing is looking for the Light.

This *whap!* can dislodge enough built-in calcification to shift your feet from unconscious wandering to firm placement upon your Path.

Which brings us to another excellent moment to engage your Retain feature. Hold your Recall Button down in the context of... remember about this *whap! Especially* remember the Awareness Possibilities it offers. Note to self: *whap!* can = wake up!

I mention the *whap!* to you now... in the context of general preparedness. So, you can "be prepared" while human. So you will have a notion. Ahhh... the *whap!*... now would be a good time to look for and connect with my enhanced Recall + Retain features. Because... let me tell you this... when you are actually in the *whap!*, it will not feel like enlightenment at all.

While in human form, it is crucial to recall that you even have a Recall Button. There will be hints and clues. The contact sequence can play something like this... you feel niggled... poked... nudged. "There's something I can't seem to recall." Niggle... a little more poke. Some prodding... niggle, niggle. "Whaaat, already?" Oh. "Could I be recalling my ability to recall?"

Traveling the eccentricities of space and time... you *will* eventually glimpse that this Recall capacity is available to you. Re-collecting. You then begin to search within yourself for ways to make good use of this capacity. Use your Recall capabilities to access insight relevant to the moment. Use your Recall + Retain functions to access Past Life Training that may prove pertinent in your current situation. Use your Recall + Retain protocols to re-collect your awareness particles.

When you find your Recall capacity... trust your ability to use it. You *do* know how. Don't gum yourself up thinking you don't. Just use it. Do it. Once you connect with your Recall capability... don't let it get dull or rusty. Use it.

While you are incarnate on Planet Earth... you absolutely do carry all of these Orientation insights within you. As you are busy being human... this may seem the farthest thing from true. I have heard human awareness likened to an extensive library. Except... oops... the library card file has been upended. Tossed about willy-nilly. All the books are there. Every reference and resource you need is in your inner library. It's just accessing those resources that may have you a bit flummoxed.

At first... should it even occur to you to look inside yourself for these insights... you will believe all is lost. Certainly not attainable. This can easily throw you into a common human rant... "God is keeping this from me! Singling me out for unfair abuse." "Everybody else knows." "God is keeping all of this from me on purpose. Just me, only me." "Oh woe. Woe is me." Whoa, indeed.

Hopefully... as you are here, now, activating this Recall + Retain feature... you will absorb and assimilate as many of these Orientation insights and clues as possible. Nail them down!

I know I've mentioned this before... but here it is again. As we are here in our current realm of pure cognizance... all is so true and apparent. Reality... so cozy. However, this "true and apparent" is substantially less obvious... definitely fogged... when you are in human form. Way foggy bottom. And what is the fog-generating machine in the incarnant realm? As you are human... you will be held captive by the nuances of your Karmic Incarnate Lessons + Loopholes... your own personal K.I.L.L. switch.

You'll spend years... decades... lifetimes... resisting... refusing... denying... your personal K.I.L.L. Tussling as if with an adversary. When really... it's only you. When really... your K.I.L.L. switch is only your own personal safety mechanism.

Eventually... shift happens. "Bring on those lessons and loopholes! Let me at 'em!" Enthusiasm = the great karmic lubricant.

Might as well be enthused, eh?

Earlier... as we began our exploration of the Human Emotional Nature... you may recall we employed an exercise... engaging with your emotion tumult and then letting it go. Caught by the turmoil. Snagged. Holding on as if it's my own. Then release. I can just let it go. Catch and release.

Practicing this exercise is a perfect moment to engage your Recall + Retain Button. One thing you *really* want to remember during your human incarnation... when it comes to the wailing tangle of your emoting self... you *can* Let It Go. The vexations want you to believe they are so important... so real. So *all*-consuming. It will not immediately occur to you that you have the option to not simply jump on the emoto train as it's racing down the track. Or... when you realize you're on that train... revved on fierce emotion... you can simply let it go. Jump off. Make a different choice. Sit down by the side of the track. Wave buh-bye as that intensity train flies by. It can happen.

Think of it as "changing channels."

Obviously, the characteristics of your Recall + Retain feature are multi-faceted. Good for so many *artifactual* transactions and states of affairs. Do yourself a favor and especially Recall + Retain the essential quality of valuing yourself and valuing others.

Another spectacular use for your Retain Button is to remember The Power of Gratitude. I know, I know... here in pure cognizant reality... you reside awash in gratitude. So, what's the big deal... right? While on Planet Earth... unless you have the supreme karmic good fortune to grow up in a host family who groks the power of gratitude... your capacity to be and feel grateful is a muscle you will need to consciously teach yourself to exercise. Remember to *feel* grateful. Don't just *think* grateful. Establish a practice of looking thru-out your Life... past, present, and future... for moments, connexions... gifts, hardships... to be grateful for. *Feel* grateful. Right now, engage your Recall + Retain Button. Remember the power of gratitude. Retain your remembering.

Gratitude lubricates the miracle.

As we wrap up this current segment on your enhancements... here is something I've got to tell you... my own personal significant suggestion. Soon, you will be standing in the "Incarnate Here" line, your travel paperwork in hand. At that time, be sure to check the boxes related to "Upgraded Time Management Skills" and "Personal Accountability." Beings who have not been in incarnation for a while may try to tell you those skills on Planet Earth are "superfluous" or "don't matter." Ha! I can't help but think... are these beings a touch arrogant, or simply misguided? Or is it that many centuries have passed on the blue-green orb since last they were in form? Humankind... its foibles... escapades... and capacities... have changed dramatically in the last few hundred years.

I will tell you from my own human experience... and especially in the context of the 21st century... you serve yourself well when you engage the capacity to navigate time. The ability to focus your thoughts... complete tasks... and hold time accountable... are totally helpful units of personal software to have installed. Some currently incarnate humans realize they missed checking those boxes before they dove into their current incarnation. They now find themselves in a human Life run amok... with challenging complications and provoking frustrations.

Yes, it's true... as you are actually incarnate human, you *can* install these time management upgrades yourself. This takes some serious effort. Major. Serious. Effort. With the thick of day-to-day Life plowing on as it does... it is a challenge for the human psyche to manage to keep up with it all. Period. In that very thick of it... it is even less likely to muster the wherewithal... to apply the required elbow grease of concentrated effort and focused intent... to alter deep-seated mental/emotional habit patterns.

Believe me, it is so much easier, and less wear-and-tear on your system in general... to simply check those boxes while you're standing in line... and come into incarnation with these operational tendencies and inclinations already installed. You will be glad you did.

Oh, hey... here's another thing. This also doesn't come from the Incarnant Prep Official Documents... but from my own experiences being human. Being fond of experimenting as I am... several of my own human Lifes ago... as I was pulling all the bits together to incarnate... I decided to stand in line 3 times as they were handing out patience. Just to see what would happen. Holy Moley! Truth be told... I have never looked back. I've stood in the pre-incarnation "Install Your Patience Here" line 3 times in a row ever since. Maximum dosage. Don't leave home without it.

Now, some incoming incarnants think, "Oh, why bother?" and they just pass by the Install Patience opportunity. No way. Experience has taught me... you simply cannot have too much patience while incarnate human on Planet Earth. Believe me... I am giving you some very useful info here.

You can't even imagine how many jagged, rough edges there are on Planet Earth... mental, emotional, and physical. So many irritants. Pesky, pesky irritants. Give yourself the innate capacity to accept and tolerate delay or trouble... without fraying into a tizzy... angry... upset. This comes in really handy. There are many annoyances, difficulties, and complaints... petty and *grande*. Interruptions. Nettles. Slow pokes. The majority of humans simply succumb to botheration and get all fussed. Agitation is not the ally it pretends to be. Standing in the steam and hassle... without getting chafed and vexed... is a quality you really want to be well-wired for.

HumanNess 101

As you are human... being able to sustain your calm composure and general tolerant nature... in the face of aggravation... will truly serve you well. Try it. Stand in that "Install Patience" line 3 times. Check it out. You'll like it. I only say that 'cause it's true.

As we now move on from HumanNess 101... you will recall our earlier demonstration which showed the Swirling Emotional Forces using and abusing a human host-expressive. Aiming to minimize this happening on your watch... your human hardware *and* software are currently being upgraded and dynamically intermeshed to allow:

The Light of Spirit to move into and thru-out you
Inspiring your awareness
Enlivening your vehicle
Having Its Uplifting Way on Planet Earth.

Your incarnate instrument is destined to be used.
Let your human self be used *that* way.

CHAPTER 5

3 Steps to Greater Awareness

"Feed that *dog."*

One spring morning in 1984, I sat meditating in our living room in Corvallis, Oregon. All of a sudden, in my head... bands of bright colors began swirling around. It was made clear to me I was being shown "emotional forces" and the compelling relationship these "forces" have within human emotional Life. Whoa! The swirling colors were so vivid... the insight so profound... my eyes popped open! Right there in my living room... those vivid bands of color continued to swirl in the air around me! I was stunned! I closed my eyes again. The colored emotional forces kept swirling in my head.

Could there be Swirling Emotional Forces active on Planet Earth? Could there be more going on here than meets the eye? Could there be *more* afoot... circulating beyond human comprehension? Yes, there definitely could be.

Could it be that we... like Mongo... are "only pawns in Game of Life?"

These swirling colors did not come alone. They brought with them a captivating realization. These emotional forces are looking for "outlets"... ways to express on Planet Earth. We humans are their "action figures"... their puppets. These emotional energy forces swirl around... just waiting for their big break. Waiting to inhabit us. Looking for a way to show up right here... in Life as we know it. We humans are the ones who allow these swirling forces to do their showing up. How else would "emotions" express on Planet Earth... if not for us humans... to spray them around?

Those Forces swirling... anger... rage... vengeance... are not going to have to wait long, as another human succumbs to vexation. Consumed. Argh! Hot under the collar. Having a conniption fit. Then, Snap! Like that! Anger has its vehicle to express in our world.

Compassion... showing up kind... the gentle heart who seeks to heal, not hurt. Caring and kindness also find expression in our world thru a person making *those* choices. Allowing *that* to be their emotional response.

I just sat there that morning... watching those swirling forces play out before me. This is a gift. A very useful piece of information. There I sat... taking it in. Absorbing the moment. Relishing. Wow.

The possibility(s) of these Emotional Forces have fascinated me ever since.

A goodly chunk of my fascination has to do with this role we humans play. How do we participate? What version of responsibility do we each have... as we allow ourselves to be the action figures of these emotional forces?

How are we... Where are we... When are we... able to take responsibility within our emotional self:

1. To have more of a say as to which emotional forces crash thru us
2. To not be victimized by our own raw emotions
3. To wield and communicate authentic, constructive emotions as we interact with Life... as we engage with the people and circumstances in our world?

We humans have this oblivious, unaware role we play so well. Numb... yet agitated. As we motivate thru our world... we fall prey to the chaos... the contusions... the trip and stumble... of our unconscious emotional Life.

Could it be that we have a more awake... more aware... more conscious... part to play?

Fascinating to consider.

I like the word "fascinating." Isn't Life fascinating?

I'm fascinated.

You've heard me say... well, you read that I wrote... I am fascinated with the nuances... the complexities... the general zaniness... of being human. How is it that we are the way we are? I have been fascinated by this for as long as I can remember. This could come from being an only child. Having lots of time to myself... to observe... mull... consider.

Fascinating that we each are who we are... with our pain and frustrations... our own self-inflicted obstacles. The things we are attracted to and interested in... our strengths and compassion. How is it that every person is wired so different... physically... emotionally... mentally? Yet, in many ways, we are so similar. How is it we humans are the way we are?

Studying The Nature of The Soul in my early 20s opened my mind in a profound manner that I had no way to anticipate. This training gave me fine gifts of insight into our many human struggles... doubts… attributes... peculiarities. Thru meditating... studying... and attending the weekly classes... I began to engage an expanding sphere of comprehension that my early 20's self had not yet realized was even available to explore.

One blossoming realization spoke clearly to me... we are each on The Path. We travel that Path with our own scenery... our obstacles... our enlightenments... and our own cast of "fascinating" characters.

The Path. My feet upon my Path. That evocative imagery has always spoken to me.

In the early years of my meditation practice, an image would come to my mind... either as I was actually meditating... or at times when I was just "daydreaming." In the image, I am taking large, rounded river rocks with both hands... lifting them down from a wall they had long been part of. I place these stones next to each other on the ground... building a road... a path. As I first began to *see* this image... rather than it just randomly running on the "background screen" of my mind... I viewed it as if standing off to one side... watching "someone" taking the stones down.

Over time... as the image would show up again... I realized that "someone" was me. I was the one lifting the stones... removing them from the wall. Placing them to make a road. In my body, I felt the weight of the stones... lifting... placing. I participated in wonder. I was "in" the movement without doubting. I did not question my actions. I am moving the stones. This is what I am doing. I am moving these stones from the wall where they have been... setting them on the ground to build a road. The day came when I completely got it. I am moving these large rocks from the wall they have been inside me. I am taking my inner wall down. Dismantling my inner obstacles to self-understanding. I am placing these stones to make a road... a path... to take me places I am meant to go.

Seeing it so clearly was a remarkable moment. This random scenario... just rambling along inside my head... showed me something I did not know how to see.

Thru this image... this "work" of moving stones from a wall to create a path... I came to realize that "something was going on" inside me. Once I grokked the significance of the image... it never randomly showed up again. Its work was done. Sure, I can conjure up the image. I did just now, to write about it. But it never randomly "showed up" the way it had before... as a revealing tool... a learning tool. A "Hey, Dana... look at this!" tool. The activity of this image showed me the movement occurring in my inner Life... before I was ever able to articulate it. Even to myself.

We each take the awareness obstacles down from within ourselves... and allow what we have learned from them to become our path to wholeness.

Each person has their own way of processing their awakening. Their own pace. Their own dance.

Each person participates in their inner transformation in their own way. This ongoing process of awakening awareness is going on in you right now. It is happening in all of us. It's why we come here to be human on Planet Earth.

3 Steps to Greater Awareness

This process... awakening to your awakening... strikes different people in different ways. Different timing. Different attributes. Different itinerary. Different reception. Some people are wary and hesitant... as their awakening begins to dawn... colliding with their view of "reality." Resist! "Whoa. Wait a minute! What's going on?"

Other folks grab this process with both hands... drawing their awakening to them. "Yes! Now! Please. Come right on in!"

My inner process shows me pictures... or I hear phrases. Sometimes, it's as if I'm being poked. Over time, I begin to recognize that an image or a thought keeps coming up. *Oh, there that is again.* Giving it some of my time... my attention... this image or phrase begins to reveal itself in ways that would not have occurred to me. It is not as if I analyze the picture or do research on the phrase. I don't "think" about it as much as I "hold" it. I look at it. I consider it. I give it my time. By "time," I don't mean 20 minutes of intense contemplation. By "time," I mean a few seconds of attention here... a few seconds there. It's almost like when you're first getting to know somebody. "Hello. Who are you?"

I do not demand the image to reveal its meaning. "Demanding" likes to think it's strong. So right. Effective. But it's not. Not really. Rather than fostering the grace of dawning realization... that "demanding" stance creates a lot of unnecessary... misguided... pressure. It's about as effective as demanding a rosebud to bloom. "Come on! Now! Blossom!"

This brings me to recall a word to the wise I read long ago... "One does not understand the beauty of a rose by examining its root under a microscope."

As I become aware of a recurring phrase or image... basically, I am curious. "Who are you *really*?" Like I said, I just "hold" this dawning realization. I "be" with it. Rather than thinking I know anything... (ha!)... I give the image or phrase an opportunity to show me what it's about.

Since my early childhood… awarenesses... processes... voices... suggestions... visuals... have just appeared in my inner world. I realize as I am writing this... how little I have thought about or questioned these suggestions and realizations. And the way they show up and play out inside me. It just happens. It just is.

For me, these inner processes are simply part of The Ride. As a child, it did not occur to me that it was unusual to have past Life experiences show up in my mind... or to hear helpful voices... or to just know something. Back in the day... it was never a good idea to tell me you had a surprise for me. My mind would show me a picture of it. This is just my normal. I'm sure it's normal for a lot of people.

3 Steps to Greater Awareness

When I was 21, my older friend Steve (he was 33) told me, "Dana, people do not experience other people the same way you do." Wow! Wow. *That* was A Moment of Revelation! I have no idea what he was seeing in me that led him to tell me this, but I instantly knew what he was talking about.

The first thought that leapt into my brain? "That explains a lot." In an instant, I was shown how I have never understood "man's inhumanity to man." Purposely inflicting pain on another person. How is this even possible? I always feel so "confronted" when witnessing meanness. Even reading about it. How in the world can you even *do* that to another human being? Might as well flail my skin and pour on the stinging vinegar. It takes my breath away. That was the first thought that came into my mind. In that moment, Steve's comment revealed to me, well... yes, that is so true. It could be that I *am* wired a little different. I never thought about it that way before.

You know how it is... you're just tootling along being you. Not giving a lot of thought to your actions and responses. It is fascinating for me as I am writing this... taking a moment to Look At these "whys and wherefores"... these "processes"... that have always percolated inside me. Taking the time to look at them in a way that allows me to describe them to you... and to myself.

Speaking of "percolate"... I have long used what I call "the percolator technique" to determine if something is really for me... or not. This can be as unremarkable as "should I buy this shirt?" In which case I would not buy it... and then see if it "percolates up." If it did, I'd go back to get it. Or I use this for something as Life-altering as deciding whether to participate in a training or to offer a meditation retreat. If something "percolates up" for me... if I find myself thinking about it, again and again... pondering it... then, okay, this must be for me. And I follow thru with it. If no "percolate"... which basically means I don't even think of it again... it must not be mine.

As I've said... thru-out my Life, I have frequently had "Previews of Coming Attractions"... realizing as something shows up in my Life, *Oh, that's just like... I have been shown this before... I've thought about that.* There are also plenty of times when A Perfectly Good Thing just happens... unannounced. Not once did I ever think about living at a Buddhist retreat center. In the Life I lived up to my early 20s... as my parent's compliant daughter... then as Bob-and-Dana... living in a Buddhist monastery was something that had never occurred to me. Not even a remote possibility.

Altho, I've got to say, since my teens, I have experienced rememberings showing me I have lived many monastic lives. One "tell" I noticed... I've always clasped my hands a certain way under a cloak or poncho as I walk. Completely unconscious. Then one day, I noticed the way I was holding my hands. Look at that. After noticing for a while... I began wondering... *Why do I hold my hands this way?* Hmmm... Giving it some consideration... over time, it eventually became clear. This way of holding my hands... clasped together over my heart center... is me walking to vespers in the chapel of a former Life.

In my early 20s... with zero fanfare in the realm of "Previews"... I found myself living at Nyingma Institute... a Tibetan Buddhist monastery in a former fraternity house in the hills of Berkeley, California. Nyingma's philosophical roots are in the Vajrayana lineage of Tibetan Buddhism. The key phrase of Vajrayana practice is... The Path Is The Goal.

You can easily imagine how captured I was by *that* phrase! The Path *IS* The Goal. Whoady Whoa! I'm lovin' that! The Path *Is* The Goal.

With The Path, itself, being The Goal... a person's perspective is truly altered. It takes the wind right out of our society's fixation on being so *Destination*-oriented. Have you noticed that happy "here and now" seems to hold very little weight, compared to happy "there and then?" I'll be happy when I get *there*. Wherever "there" may be. I can't possibly be happy *now*... I have to graduate from college first... then I'll be happy. I want to have a baby... then I'll be happy. I have to own my own house... get a great job... have my first art exhibit... *then* I'll be happy.

How is it we think of so many reasons to put off being happy?

There you are putting off being happy... the tricky thing is... Life goes on and on. A person graduates from college... are you happy now? "Are you kidding? Now I have to find a job! The competition is fierce. I really should buckle down and get into grad school." You have had your first baby... Congratulations! Now are you happy? "OMG! I'm exhausted. Totally sleep-deprived. This is so much work. It's *constant*!" You own a lovely home... happy now? "It's always something... crabgrass... plumbing... rewiring... we need more furniture... the backyard needs work. Happy? Are you kidding?! I'm overwhelmed."

It is, indeed... always something. That is the title of Gilda Radner's engaging and poignant autobiography... *It's Always Something*. And it always *will* be "something." There will always be some "good reason" to put off being happy. Not just yet. No. Wait. I can't be happy. Not right now.

You're doing yourself a big favor as you take a look at "All the Reasons I Cannot Be Happy Now." Get a handle on these self-justifications holding off happy. Don't let "not now" run away with you and your Life. Sit down. Make a list. Be real with yourself. What keeps you from being happy? What are your "reasons"… your "excuses?" And these excuses get to win because…?

This is so worth taking a look at. Why, exactly, is it that I cannot be happy now? What am I telling myself? So worth listening. So worth changing.

Over 20 years ago, came a random realization that totally rearranged my perception molecules. One day, as I was musing to myself, I somehow wandered into the realm of "going out of this incarnation." Musing along… imagining I was "leaving"… I turned and looked back at my Life. In that moment, insight flashed… I don't want to go out of incarnation, look back at my Life, and say, "Darn, I meant to be happy!" "I went to Planet Earth and I forgot to be happy!" Whoa. Wait. That's not right. A moment of amazing realization. As the years have moved on… there are times I revisit that Aha!… and see what a completely pivotal moment it was for me. All of a sudden, I saw the living of my Life from a very different orientation.

I meant to be happy.

"Happy" doesn't necessarily mean sex, booze, rock'n'roll… party, party, party all night long. Obviously, "happy" means different things to different people. In the context of a Life well-lived… "happy" means being at peace within yourself and within your Life. Genuinely glad. Seeing the grace in everyday Life. Being satisfied with who you are... what you've got... and the contribution you are making to your world.

"Being satisfied" brings me back to living at Nyingma. An experience of major, Life-enhancing proportions. Very ordinary in the day-to-day... tasks... chores... service. The completely extraordinary part was living in such a reverent environment. An environment that valued the sacred. A blessing to me in so many different ways. My heart... my knowing... my awareness... developed in ways I could have never imagined.

My very first day at Nyingma could easily have been enough. As a new arrival, I was being shown around the building. My guide brought me to the open door of the library where the Rinpoche, Tarthang Tulku, was speaking to a group of people. In Tibetan Buddhism... Rinpoche (RIN poe shay) is an honorific title given to a highly respected religious teacher. It literally means Precious One.

Standing in the doorway... I heard Rinpoche say, "The only difference between an enlightened person and an unenlightened person is a sense of satisfaction. That is the only difference." Really? Well... there you go! Thank you for that totally worthwhile piece of information. It is obvious I immediately made note... because here I am, over 40 years later... sharing this fate-full moment with you.

I was just "randomly" standing in that doorway. Standing there as he "happened" to say... as he happened to hand me a Life-altering clue. Satisfaction. I have reflected on this comment *many* times over the years. I've shared it with a lot of different people. The "only difference." Being satisfied. That simple.

Maybe not that simple. It seems satisfaction is not a human being's "natural state." Simply content... satisfied... with what you have and who you are. Oh, come on! Seeking enlightenment has got to be more strenuous than that!

Fulfilled. Gratified. Check it out. Nothing reveals the possibilities more clearly than exploring for yourself. Give yourself a moment. What would it feel like to be satisfied? Fulfilled. Deeply satisfied within yourself. Satisfied with your Life. Satisfied with your decisions and choices. Satisfied with your outcomes. Satisfaction. How does that feel? Give it to yourself. Rinse and repeat. Practice. Give yourself to satisfaction. Practice some more.

Experiment. Let yourself *feel* satisfied. Investigate. Breathe in satisfied. Centered within... I am satisfied. Smear satisfied around inside yourself. Let your heart feel satisfied. Exhale satisfied into your world. Sit with it. Evaluate.

Some might say, "I can't be satisfied... I'll lose my edge!" "I might become complacent." "My dissatisfaction motivates me!"

Okay. I am only suggesting an experiment. Try on satisfaction. See how it fits. Observe what happens.

Now, in my later years... I am more awed than ever that I got to live at Nyingma just as I was stepping into my adult Life. During my months there, I occasionally participated in meditation retreats. Much more of the time, I worked as part of the staff... at the reception desk... doing registration for seminars. Or occupied in the kitchen... cooking, serving, cleaning up. While I was there... both thru my own retreat experience... and as I observed others experiencing their mindfulness practice... I came to know the value of silence. The value of mindful awareness. The value of being in this moment now.

The deep, centered experience of mindfulness... mindful walking... mindful eating... mindful breath.

Being aware *in* the actual experience of what I am doing.

Release chatter. In the Now. Be in *this* step. Let go of distraction. Make the choice.

Focus my wandering mind. Lucid. Here. Now.

Be in *this* breath. This awareness. This silence. This practice.

It touched me, deep and profound. Amazing nourishment. Resonant deep within me. I know the value of this. I've done this before.

Be present... within this bite. This chew. This swallow.

In the early 2000s, Scott and I participated in a day of mindfulness practice with the revered Buddhist monk and peace activist Thich Nhat Hanh. In the course of the day, we were offered an approach to mindful eating that was different than the way I'd learned at Nyingma. Before we ate... Thich Nhat Hanh spoke... encouraging us to contemplate where our food had come from. Mindfully connecting with and thanking the person who planted and nurtured the seed... the person who harvested the food... the person who transported it. With each bite... acknowledging and appreciating the person who prepared what I am eating... the person who packaged it... the one who served it to me.

This quality of mindfulness... tho different from the way I learned... is certainly equally valid. Its gift is a gentle, humbling awareness of the interconnectedness of all things. The Web of Life.

Oh... and by the way... I'm not going to sit here and tell you... mindfulness practice is *so easy*. It's not. At first.

Just as with satisfaction... silence and mindfulness are not a human's "natural state." Or... hey... perhaps they are more our natural state than we realize. This human journey we're on is just so darn fascinating with its curves and chaos. Maybe running around all crazed... annoyed and anxious... is *not* our "natural state." In fact... we do have other possibilities. With intention... patience... and willing, conscious choice... we begin to uncover these natural gems of being. Mindfulness. Inner peace. Fulfillment. We then gift them to ourselves. Maybe *that's* the way it is. All more natural than we have ever realized.

Of course, not so easy "at first" would be the operative words here. Before judging whether you are *able* to give these deepening experiences to yourself... give yourself some time to settle in to the practice. The possibilities. Each of us being wired differently as we humans are... there are some folks who welcome mindfulness with a warm embrace = At Last. Others find it more of a struggle... and succumb to holding it away. If you are drawn to mindfulness... silence... satisfaction... your very interest will guide you to ways you can give such treasures to yourself.

It's not that anyone has it "more together" or "less together" than anybody else. We're all just different.

My first encounters with mindfulness came a couple of years before my time at Nyingma. In my early 20s, I lived at Well-Springs, a retreat center in the Santa Cruz Mountains, south of San Francisco. Well-Springs offered a program "that transforms energy thru the integration of the Arts and Spirituality." In a peaceful mountain setting with a cathedral of magnificent fir trees and sweet, gentle breezes, an incredible British woman named Kay Ortmans utilized a synthesis of art, movement, classical music, and massage to facilitate healing. I was introduced to Kay and Well-Springs by Geri House, a dear, older woman who was a student in the first Nature of The Soul class I taught.

Thru Well-Springs' program of integrative creativity, I was given my initial opportunities... to be mindful... silent... open to awareness. I found sometimes I could really let go and *be* in the experience. Centered. Silent. Home.

Other times, it took so much *effort* to stay focused and silent. I was jumping all around inside myself... like I had the heebie-jeebies. I just wanted to get *out* of there!

Similar to Nyingma... as I lived at Well-Springs... there were days when I participated in retreat programs... and other days I was staff. I remember one time... I was part of a group doing a day-long silent retreat. Turns out, this was one of my "efforting" days. I was not all engaged and easy with it. Several hours into being silent... I happened to overhear that one of my favorite coworkers was driving into town to do some shopping. Holy Cows! "Wait for me!" It was definitely not "good form" for me to split, but I couldn't help myself. I couldn't get out of there fast enough! I told a friend on staff, "I have to go buy a toothbrush." I jumped in the truck and off we drove! I was euphoric. Those trees never looked more beautiful. The air never smelled so sweet. I'm free!

Free to do what?

We're so used to talking whenever and wherever we please. And talking some more. It can be a challenge... boy, I'll say!... to be silent. It feels unnatural. To simply not talk... is not that simple. Okay... well it *is* simple. It's just not that easy.

I remember the sense I felt as I milled around town: "Ahhhh... normal." As if I had escaped. I didn't really even talk to anyone. But, I could have if I'd wanted to! I didn't *have to* be silent. As days went by... I would look back at my "escape." I found myself wondering... *escape from what? Escape to what? What exactly is "normal?" What exactly is "escape?"*

Sometimes, as you begin to practice silence or mindfulness, you'll want to jump right out of your skin. That's okay. Really. Remember... this is exercise. Stretching. Exploring. You do not have to be perfectly silent immediately. Perfectly mindful. There is no "immediately" requirement. No Rule #42: "Must be totally good at mindful on first try." Nope. No such thing. Give your fine self a break. You're beginning. Learning. Unwinding.

You've spent the first 20... 30... 50... years of your Life spinning on your inner hamster wheel... chattering away... thoughts racing. Silence does not just happen. That doesn't mean you shouldn't do it. Give it a stretch. Your mindfulness muscles are completely worth exercising.

Vast and amazing benefit shows up as you practice mindfulness. A gift of grace reveals itself. A certain deep magic. As you settle quietly within. Release yourself to the experience.

Any spiritual practice is far deeper than it appears to be on the surface. Mindfulness opens realms of awareness you don't even realize are inside you.

The important thing to grasp about spiritual practice is the *Experience* of it. An experience that *you give yourself to*. Meditation. Chanting. Mindfulness. You surrender. Let go. Allow.

You're not thinking about doing it. You're doing it.

You're not thinking about having the experience. You're experiencing.

You are in it. It is in you. All in.

Let's consider the *experience* of chanting. Chanting is not to be confused with singing hymns. Not for a moment am I saying one religious tradition is "better" or "lesser" than any other. Just different. Western religious traditions have a more cerebral relationship with God... singing about God... God does this... God does that. Or beseeching God... God, please do this... please do that. The Eastern traditions give devotion a different spin. Singing *to* God. Yay God! Celebrating God. Hare Krishna = Yay God!! Govinda Jiya Jiya = God! Yay! Yay!

Ahhhh... chanting. You chant for the joy of chanting. You give yourself to chanting. Chanting gives itself to you.

Chanting snuck up on me.

Pure wonderment.

In my teens and 20s, I sang in several choirs... high school choir... church choirs... community chorale groups. A few years after the fact, I realized that "Dona Nobis Pacem" was my first chant. I learned "Dona Nobis Pacem" as I sang alto in the Unitarian Church choir in downtown Los Angeles. We were called "The Ensemble"... a much cooler name for "choir." And cool we were. Along with the music, there was dance and "production." Not inclined to stand in one place, we choreographed. Sometimes, we'd be sitting around in the congregation... beginning to sing, we'd stand up and walk to the front. It was the early 70s. This was quite rad. Our eclectic performances often included the brass quartet or strings from the L.A. Philharmonic or The Music Center. Much fine musical creativity transpired.

As I sang "Dona Nobis Pacem," I didn't think of it as "a chant." Altho chant it I did... especially as I was driving.

A couple years after The Ensemble, I learned my first Sanskrit chant. Traveling with a group of folks in the back of a VW van, we chanted "Hare Krishna" as we plowed thru snowstorms in the Siskiyou Mountains on our way from Oregon to Southern California. One heckuva magical mystery tour.

A few weeks later, came an experience that unexpectedly revealed to me a deep truth about chanting. I was driving to a party. The only person I would know there was the host. I had all sorts of mental garbage going on... *Nobody's going to like you. This is going to be miserable. You won't find anybody to connect with.* On and on. *You might as well turn around and go home. This will be terrible. Forget about it!* Mental garbage on full churn.

I kept trying to ease out of this state... to straighten myself around. Driving along, my mind would show me past times when I hadn't known anybody at a party and I'd had a fine time. *Remember that time at Kassie's... you didn't know anyone... and you met Martin... and Brandy. It turned out great.* The onslaught of putrid mental gunk was not going to give up easily. It hammered on and on. Finally, I shouted at myself, "Just stop thinking about it!" To which my thinkery flashed, "If I don't think about that then what *am* I going to think about?"

My mind began to chant... *Hare Krishna... Hare Rama...*

I didn't think, *I'm going to chant*. Chanting arrived on its own.

Total revelation! The wonder of my mind starting to chant completely turned me around. Of course! Chanting filled my mental space. My negative thoughts released their strangle-hold on me. Poop silenced. Garbage gone. I was in awe how chanting fixed me. *This* is what chanting is about?! Excellent.

Chanting freed me from my own mental badgering. Instead of stinkin' thinkin' grinding away making me miserable... my heart lifted... I soared as I sang. Smiling, I proceeded to my friend's house. Chanting all the way. Freed from continuing to wallow in doubt and self-inflicted ridiculousness. (I had a good time.)

Chanting intervened.

The inner shift that came with this miraculous moment did more than free me from my negative self-talk. It also showed me more than I *ever* imagined about the grace... the power... of chanting. Not because I dissected my doubt and fear and "figured it out." But because chanting busted thru... scattered my stinkin' thinkin'... centered my heart and mind. Here Dana... this is what chanting is about. Woo Hoo! When you are victimized by hurtful, self-limiting clatter that you don't want to continue flailing yourself with... chant instead. Chanting is not thinking. Chanting operates at a completely different place inside you.

Letting go into chanting, you embrace the perfect consort to bring yourself into this present moment. Let's establish a degree of self-civility here... shall we?

As you begin to chant... put distraction aside. Lift your heart and mind. Release yourself more fully into your Spiritual Life. Allow the deep, resonant tones of the chant to pour thru you. Give it to yourself. Give yourself to it. Chant for the chanting. Chant. Don't try to direct it. Allow it to show you the way. Release yourself to the experience. See where chanting takes you.

Don't muck yourself up with over-think. There you are... busy... thinking about meditation. Thinking about chanting. Thinking about mindfulness. Thinking about silence. Thinking about doing it right. Thinking about how you can't do it. Thinking will always try to convince you how *important* it is to think. Do yourself a favor. Release yourself from the self-imposed limitations of over-think-o-rama.

Thinking about meditation and actually meditating are 2 very different things. Thinking about silence and residing in silence are 2 very different things. Be willing to explore the wealth of possibilities. Stretch. Yoga for the mind. Give yourself to the Experience. Give the Experience to yourself.

The gifts of mindful awareness are vast and profound. Truthfully... you have no idea these gifts exist or how they will touch you until you actually let go and embrace experiencing them. Many people are immediately in judgment... ready to find fault with something unknown or unfamiliar. Other people are totally... "Where have you been all my Life?"

With chanting and meditation... don't pretend you understand it until you actually *do* it. Until you make yourself accessible... approachable. Reachable. Teachable.

As with many of Life's profound gifts... the gifts of mindfulness are known only as you let go. Surrender. Give yourself to *this* moment.

Based on how deeply I value these *experiences* of silence, of mindfulness and meditation... these practices are, of course, integrated into my Women's Spirit Circles and Retreats. During a retreat... we eat lunch mindfully... in silence. At a one-day Women's Spirit Retreat I offered in Southern California... I invited the women to be silent... mindful... as they ate their lunch. As the talking stick passed around the Circle at the end of the day... one woman let it be known... she did NOT like being silent at lunch. She did not like it at all. Even after a day of gentle practice... she managed to be in a huff about it.

A few weeks later, she sought me out. "I apologize for making a fuss because I didn't like you having us eat our lunch in silence. I get it now. Truly profound. Thank you." We each have our own experience.

Practicing silence and mindfulness *can* be easy. Simple. Rewarding. Exercise *those* muscles. Once you get the hang of it... once you give yourself to it... mindfulness is a very yummy thing. Nourishing.

Mindfulness is its own brand of quiet exhilaration.

~~~ ~~~ ~~~

During my childhood and thru my teens... it was as if I had "an etheric pouch"... an invisible "pocket"... in place at the top of my right thigh. As I moved thru those years... "pieces of the puzzle" would randomly show up in my Life. I had no idea what puzzle. Or why this was "a piece." I just knew it was. As I would have an experience... or hear a phrase... there would be a particular "shimmer" to it. I realize, looking back at it now... I didn't question the shimmer. Noticing it, I would think, *Ah, there's that shimmer.* I would take that experience or phrase... that "piece"... and place it in my "pouch." This was another of my inner processes that I didn't really question. I didn't give it a lot of attention. I just did it. *Oh look, there's that shimmer*... put it in my "pocket."

I clearly remember one of these "pieces." When I was 15, soon to get my driver's license, my parents arranged a private driving instructor for me. Three times a week, a white sedan... equipt with 2 steering wheels, 2 sets of brakes and 2 accelerators... would show up at my house. Off we'd go. My driving teacher, Ed, was a really nice guy. One time, while we were driving, he told me that he had wanted to be a brain surgeon. But he fell in love, got married, and immediately had 5 kids. So, now he was teaching people how to drive.

Our first time out driving together… Ed asked me to make a left turn from San Fernando Road, over the railroad tracks, onto Hollywood Way. This was a very wide intersection. As I was making the left turn, I intended to straighten into my lane and drive on. However… I was looking at the car I was about to drive past and I started veering toward it. Ed deftly adjusted his steering wheel to avoid a collision. As we continued driving down Hollywood Way, calmly looking straight ahead, he said, "Dana, don't look at what you don't want to hit." Shimmer. Uh huh. That makes sense. Don't look at where you *don't* want to go… 'cause you'll just take yourself there. I didn't analyze or dissect his comment. I just put that "piece" of useful information in my "pocket."

"Don't look at what you don't want to hit." Such a helpful suggestion. We humans do tend to fixate on the thing we "don't want to hit." Worrying. Anxious about the outcome. Troubled that things are going to turn out "wrong." Fixated… we steer ourselves right toward it.

Moving into my adult Life, I became a tad obsessed with exercising my "don't worry" muscles. One of my ongoing "Life lessons" has been tight money. In my early 20s… living on my own after splitting from Bob... I'd get so bummed when I had to use gift money (birthday, Christmas) to pay the electric bill. Sure, it was nice to have money to pay the bill. But what a poo, not being able to spend the money as it was intended. Oh, you know... on a gift for myself.

Tight money is a serious kind of strenuous. I know this does not come as news. Concern and conflict about money tears apart families... marriages... businesses... friendships. Having stewed and fretted about money worries... freaking myself out numerous times... I realized, in my later 20s... "anxiety does not pay the bills." I could be anxious and concerned... uptight all I wanted to be about a past-due bill. But that worry only made me miserable. It sure didn't get the bill paid.

"Anxiety does not pay the bills" became a mantra of mine. Reminding myself to not get all worked up about it. Dana... stewing gets you nowhere. Just figure out a way to pay the bills.

My *"A #1 Best"* don't-worry mantra came to me one evening in Portland, Oregon, standing near the corner of Sandy Blvd and Burnside... waiting for the signal to change. I was standing at a little side street. It was a long light. I stood there for a while. Across the street... right in front of me... an electronic sign streamed events and information for a church on that corner. I stood there waiting... occasionally glancing at the yadda yadda on the streaming billboard. Waiting. Waiting. Just before the light changed, I saw these words stream by: "... paid in advance on a debt you may never owe." Say what? What was that about?

When the signal changed... rather than crossing the street... I stood there waiting for the sign to cycle thru all its info again. When it finally did... I read "Worry is interest, paid in advance, on a debt you may never owe." Holy cow! Taking pen and paper out of my purse... I stood on that street corner until the sign went thru its whole cycle again. I wrote that insightful piece of information down. Wowza! Such a great way to say it.

Over the years, I have exercised that one A Lot. Being a former bank employee... I really got it. Interest paid in advance on *a debt you may never owe*. Here you've stewed and fretted... putting all of this anxious energy into being concerned... fearful... for yourself... for someone else's well-being. Worrying over an outcome. And then, *voila!*... 9.5 times out of 10, everything turns out fine. There you've burned all that time and energy... all those anxiety calories... churning in worry. You've "paid all that interest"... "in advance"... and everything turns out fine. Just Fine.

Worry is not the ally it pretends to be. Worry gets you all worked up. Freaked out. Then none of the dreadful stuff you were stewing about happens. You're stewed.

I'm on a mission... let's just eliminate that ol' worry honcho.

As I mentioned earlier... I frequently create "party favors" to share with my Women's Spirit Circles. Many times, these are printed hand-outs... with uplifting, relevant information... or quotes I like. Useful stuff. Years ago... in service to my mission of releasing us all from the anxiety scoundrel... I created a half-sheet on card stock with some of my favorite worry quotes. It is titled:

What, Me Worry!?!

Worry is interest, paid in advance,
on a debt you may never owe.

Worry does not empty tomorrow of its sorrow;
it empties today of its strength. ~ Corrie Ten Boom

If I spent as much time doing the things
I *worry* about getting done
as I do worrying about doing them,
I wouldn't have anything to worry about. ~ Unknown

Do not worry about tomorrow,
for tomorrow will worry about itself.
Each day has enough trouble of its own. ~ Matthew 6:34

Remember, today is the tomorrow
you worried about yesterday. ~ Dale Carnegie

> It is not work that kills men, it is worry.
> Work is healthy;
> you can hardly put more on a man than he can bear.
> But worry is rust upon the blade.
> It is not movement that destroys the machinery,
> but friction. ~ Henry Ward Beecher

> If you believe that feeling bad or worrying long enough
> will change a past or future event,
> then you are residing on another planet
> with a different reality system. ~ William James

> Worry is a thin stream of fear
> trickling through the mind.
> If encouraged it cuts a channel into which
> all other thoughts are drained. ~ Arthur Somers Roche

> Don't Worry. Be Happy. ~ Meher Baba

Meher Baba (1894-1969) was a revered Indian spiritual master. I was in my early 20s, the first time I saw a little poster with Meher Baba's face and... "Don't worry. Be happy." I immediately thought of the tag line of Mad Magazine's Alfred E. Neuman: "What, me worry?!" I'm sure Alfred E. was responding to Meher Baba's sage words of advice.

Then there's the Arthur Somers Roche quote right above Meher Baba's... "Worry is a thin stream of fear trickling through the mind. If encouraged, it cuts a channel into which all other thoughts are drained." The visual of that really captured me... I could *see* that "thin stream trickling... cutting a channel" and all those other thoughts "draining into it." Mesmerizing. How totally effective that is.

As time went on... I created a variation... my own version. "Gratitude is a thin stream of Love trickling through the mind. If encouraged, gratitude cuts a channel into which all other thoughts are drained." Love cuts a channel into which all other thoughts are drained. Let's go there.

And where would we be without those well-worn variations on the theme of worry... shoulda... woulda... coulda? Worry's triplet cousins. We spin ourselves like a top. I should have... I would have... I could have... "I should have said something smart." "I would have done it if given half a chance." "I could have built that." We are the star in our ongoing, wrenching mental scenarios of discontent. And yet, under a degree of scrutiny... even as crazed as we make ourselves... it turns out shoulda... woulda... coulda... doesn't make a Life. They're just whining about Life.

This litany of discontent whirs along in the background of our mental jungle gym. Reminding us of the ways we have been wronged... where our shortfalls are... and how much everything costs.

This disgruntled fog persists as we hunger for... we know not what. What is this ache... this deep, unfulfilled yearning? Yearning for *what*? This is what I call the nebulous gnaws. The simmering discontent that gnaws away inside. The spin cycle. Perpetual internal agitation. Stewing fragments of dissatisfaction. Making me see my Life as not right... not okay... not enough. Nebulous as all get-out. Wispy. Dim. Hidden in the rush of inner chatter. These disgruntled mental murmurings don't even completely register. Surprising how effective they are... spreading discontent as they fester away inside. Our emotions hear these grumblings. Our hearts believe them. We feel bad. It hurts to be me.

Our emotions hear our negative self-talk even when we don't. Self-defeating mental grumble makes itself a background mantra. Awash in our general mental cacophony... we don't even consciously notice this continual spew of negative self-talk. But we do begin to *feel*... down, defeated, sad... angry, anxious, steamed. We feel "put upon" long before we even notice that we are "putting upon" ourselves. We can't feel better about Life and living until we hear the self-defeating mutter we're berating ourselves with. Hear it and change it. Because we can.

Thru the early 2000s, Scott and I offered our own Sunday Service in the North Hollywood/Toluca Lake area of Southern California. For me, this was *deja vu* all over again. I had attended Toluca Lake Elementary School... and for decades, my mom worked at the Bank of America in Toluca Lake, right across from the entrance to Warner Brothers Studios. When Bob and I were married, our apartment was in North Hollywood. Here I am again.

In the different church communities we'd been involved with thru the years... I've always especially liked when guest speakers spoke on Sunday morning. Each speaker with their own style... their own emphasis... their own way. So, when we had our own congregation... we frequently invited guest speakers to present their way... their message... at our Sunday Service.

One Sunday, our guest speaker spoke of Higher Consciousness... Nirvana... Greater Awareness... as if we were all already there. Near the end of her talk, from the back of the room... I heard Sharon, one of our regulars, mutter... "Yeah, that's great, but how do we get there?"

Her sincerity, the pain in her voice touched me. I thought, *Good question*. Hers became the question I could not get out of my head. "How do we get there?" The next day, I sat myself down to give this some thought. How *do* we get there? What do we need to figure out... about ourselves and about Life... that would bring us to a peaceful place of centered, assured clarity within?

I pondered. The first thing that came to me was… we humans are continually victimized by our own negative self-talk. And we don't even know it. We don't consciously realize the simmering stew… the spew… of self-defeating, ugly, unkind mental regurgitation we fester in. Top billing… playing day in and day out… behind the scenes of our conscious awareness.

"I'm stupid, fat, and ugly." "No one will ever take me seriously." "He's never going to like me." "I don't know what I'm doing." "I'm such a loser." These thoughts tumble around… grumble around. Simmering in our inner crockpot. We rarely even hear them. We're so used to this spew of negative self-talk… it barely registers.

But, here's the tricky thing… thru our subconscious mind, our emotions pick up this stinky talk. It does register there. Our feelings respond accordingly. We walk around feeling… down… angry… put upon… anxious… discouraged. Our emotions believe and "emote" according to these thought-triggers we don't even hear ourselves muttering.

We walk around in a fog of self-disgust and anxiety that we have no clue we are self-generating. We usually perceive our pain and botheration as someone else's "fault." "He makes me so mad!" "She hurt my feelings." When presented with the possibility that we, ourselves, are generating our fear, pain, and anxiety... our first response is a heated, "I am not! It's *their* fault!"

Okay.

Drawing a deep breath, I become aware of what I am telling myself. I take a moment to hear my own mental mantra. I open to being aware of what I am telling myself in this moment. Always a good first step. Useful. Worthwhile. At first blush, so simple... I am listening to my inner conversation.

Further exploration reveals that hearing what you say to yourself is trickier than it may sound. Tricky... slippery... and harsh. As you begin to hear your inner commentator, you can't help but notice your tone of voice as you talk with yourself. Disgusted. Mean. Unkind. I've mentioned before, and it's worth repeating… if you talked to your friends the way you talk to yourself... you wouldn't have any friends.

As I contemplate Sharon's question, it's pretty clear to me... Step One: Listen to Your Thoughts.

Listen to your thoughts. Become aware of the way you talk to yourself. So you can change it. So you can evolve the way *you* communicate with *you*.

Now, what else do we need to figure out as we find our way to Greater Awareness?

Let's look at that tendency toward self-harshness. Such a buzz-kill. Highly likely it will raise its snarling head as we continue our inner quest. Like a pro... we pick, pick, pick on ourselves. And, of course, who wouldn't? Look at... "All of the things about me that are so not enlightened." We become riveted by our flaws... our weaknesses... all that is "not right." "Enlightened? Ha! Look at all my sicko stuff! I am so messed up."

As you travel your Path... harshness is not the ally it pretends to be.

Delving deeper within... authentic and honest with yourself... the best companion you can bring along with you is self-kindness. Without a healthy dose of self-kindness, your inner journey to awareness becomes mired in self-abuse. You deserve better.

Self-kindness?

What? The inner voice who judges you so harshly is stunned! Self-kindness? Are you kidding me?!

Self-kindness is a path so less-traveled... it takes a moment or 3 to adjust.

Contemplating self-kindness... I remembered... when I was a kid, one of "my voices" had something to say about that. This was a distinctly female voice. Every now and then... out of the blue... she would say, "Be kind to yourself, Sister. Be kind." I could almost see her. She had brown hair. I was struck by the way she called me "Sister." As an only child in this Life... technically, I am nobody's "sister." Yet she knew me as sister. I always appreciated the kind, encouraging quality of her voice.

Self-kindness? Really? Yup.

As you travel along your spiritual path... self-kindness is a stunningly effective Life-strategy.

Self-kindness is the healing balm that lifts and transforms your awareness.

Who knew?

As I mentioned earlier... this miraculous Life possibility crept up on me many years ago, as I sat meditating. I was sending kindness from my heart out to friends... family... and fellow humans. This was a regular practice of mine. It feels great... pouring kindness out to others.

To revisit this particular experience... totally unbidden by me... the stream of kindness flowing out turned and came right back into *my* heart! Gasp! *You mean kindness is not just to send* out*? I can send kindness to* myself*?!*

Truly, a radical notion! It took the wind right out of me.

Recovering... I closed my eyes again. What's going to happen now? My heart loves pumping kindness. I experimented. Toward myself. Receiving. Gently feeling this kindness filling my heart. Holding. Breathing. Allowing. Allowing myself to *believe* this kindness directed to myself. It was A Moment. I sat. Breathing. Holding. Marveling. Even tho it had never occurred to me before... it rang so true.

In the months before this "kindness boomerang" shot back into my heart… I'd begun noticing that thru all of my meditating years… I was like a bulldog with a bone. Grabbing onto Spirit. Grrrrr. I was in a tussle. I began to realize that I "pulled." I struggled. I definitely efforted. Drawing Light and Soul Consciousness into my awareness… I pulled hard. There was definitely grunt involved. I worked it… hard.

I began to glimpse that grunt. Whoa. Really? Grunting? Grrrrr. Is that what this is all about? Grunting? Struggling? Then… as I was really seeing it… I began thinking… *why am I doing this to myself? Why am I doing it this way? Why grunt? Why harsh and mean? Why jerking on it so hard?* Like maybe I won't get it? Like maybe I don't deserve spiritual awareness unless I grab on really hard? Unless I tussle? Grrrrr.

Finally noticing all of my grunt and struggle… searching for another "way"… I came up with the phrase… "My Soul's *Loving* Intent." A captivating shift from "My Soul's thou-shalt-not-be-deemed-worthy-unless-you-grunt-really-hard Intent." I reached upward… lifting my heart and mind… aligning with and welcoming my Soul's *loving* intent. From a grunting bull dog to a gentler, kinder version of me becoming more aware. A whole new world awoke within.

I see now that this profound shift in my awareness…

from grunt to uplift... was "tilling the soil"... so this Wave of Kindness *could* turn around and come back into my heart. As my awakening process continued... I was cultivating a heart environment of fresh, moist, nurturing soil... rather than one that was hard, dry, compacted.

As you begin to wake up... a whole new world appears. Giving yourself the time to embrace love... clear vision... compassion... you begin to perceive the Loving Guidance that is always and already available to you. Turn your attention to it. You begin growing your awareness by giving it some consideration. By giving it your time. Your thought energy. Your gratitude.

Take a moment to acknowledge that you have a spiritual body. "Hello, spiritual body." Your spiritual body is the very foundation of your instrument. Your animating Life force. As it infuses all of your being... this is the framework your mental, emotional, and physical bodies are hung upon. Your Life begins in your spiritual essence and radiates... thru your thoughts... your feelings... your actions and expression... out into your world.

Just as you exercise your physical body... express your emotional self... and come up with new, creative thoughts and ideas... you can also exercise and fortify your spiritual body. A good start is simply acknowledging that your spiritual self exists. It is as much a part of you as your hair...

your toes... your laugh. *This...* your spiritual body... is your Life ally.

Meditation is excellent exercise for your spiritual self. As you meditate, you get to know all of yourself better. You come to know your spiritual self. It already knows you.

Again, let me say... your Life is about what you give your attention to. This can be a slippery concept. Yet, so worth grabbing hold of. You grow the different aspects of your Life as you give your attention to them. No attention = no growth. When you think about it... this seems so obvious. Yet slippery. Take a few moments to give attention to your thoughts. What are you thinking about right now? Energy follows thought. What are you telling yourself? It can be challenging to actually focus on where your attention resides. Or where it is flitting about. Many times, we don't even realize... yucky things that show up in Life come about because we've been giving them our thought energy. Our attention.

Here we have yet another advantage to listening to your thoughts... you become more aware of just what is receiving your attention. Give your attention to "what I am grateful for"... rather than "what I resent." It changes the way you see things. It changes the way you are in your Life.

As Mr. Incredible laments... "I was so obsessed with feeling undervalued, I undervalued all of you." That's an

3 Steps to Greater Awareness

inner maneuver worth noticing.

Choosing to apply self-kindness and turning your attention to what you are telling yourself... you become more engaged... more awake and aware... more alive in your Life. This isn't a game of spiritual hide-and-seek we're playing here. The Game is one of you directing your own attention... growing your own awareness of Love... waking up within yourself.

Game on!

This Game gives you the opportunity to discover a new group of muscles. Your gratitude muscle. Your awareness muscle. Your self-compassion muscle. Your *responding*-in-this-moment-rather-than-reacting muscle. Each of these muscles is an intriguing part of your anatomy. Begin actively exercising *those* muscles. Experiment. What happens when I exercise my self-compassion muscle? When I exercise the muscle that sees what is right in my Life rather than focusing on what's wrong? What happens when I give my attention to my gratitude muscle?

Exercising these awareness muscles will have you choosing to look in that direction. You give these upgrade possibilities your attention. Hmmmm... self-kindness... self-compassion. This shift in what you give your attention to takes you to new realms... ones that exist beyond same-ol'... same-ol' you.

When you choose to look in this new direction... you find the grace that is self-kindness. The awesome, clarifying power of self-kindness releases you from your own inner neglect and abuse. Relating to yourself... without over-moralizing... without harshness... you release yourself from the self-limiting distractions of shame and inner conflict. You unfetter yourself as you realize you *can* let go of these hurtful, self-imposed distractions.

So, as we continue along this Path of "Yeah, but how do we get there?"... Step Two: Self-Kindness.

It seems most of us grow up believing we have to be harsh and impatient with ourselves. Yes, this could be a carry-over from the way we were spoken to in childhood by parents... other adults... older siblings. Listening to your thoughts... hearing what you say to yourself... and *how you say it*... gives you the option to treat your self better. Exercising your self-kindness muscle frees your conscious awareness to move far beyond your self-inflicted limitations. Thank Goodness for that.

Listening to your thoughts and exercising Self-Kindness = excellent movement in the right direction.

As I continued to ponder Sharon's question... I realized there is a third step. This takes us full circle. Right to where we want to be.

Step Three: Appreciation.

Gratitude. Seeing Life's Blessings. Thank you. *Mahalo. Gracias, Amigo.*

Here's the deal... it's ALL here ALL the time... poopiness, despair, vexation, anxiety... uplift, laughter, hope, health, peace. It is ALL here ALL the time.

What do you choose to look at? What do you choose to see? Where does your attention go? What do you tend to talk about? How do you tend to talk about it? What's "real" for you?

As I mentioned earlier... your Life is the story you are telling yourself inside your own head. The story of your happy childhood... or how miserable you were. The story of how you are treated in your Life. Your story of slights and abuse... of opportunities and recognition. The story of your circumstances. Your fate. Your successes. Your failures. The story of how you look. How you are. The impact you're having in your world. Or not.

What is the story you are telling yourself?

As I was growing up, I was often told, "Count your blessings." This was usually delivered more as a rebuke than a helpful suggestion. Turns out to be a pertinent bit of advice. Several times in the later 80s, I read or heard, "Before you go to sleep at night... think of 3 things you are grateful for." After that suggestion had popped up a number of times here and there, I thought, *Okay, sure, I can do that.*

Before falling asleep at night, I'd take a moment to "think of 3 things"... my kids... meditation... the sunset... friendships... realizations. I like this. It's an enjoyable thing to do. This "I am grateful for..." practice came with its own surprise. It didn't take long to realize... the more I took time to notice and express my gratitude... the more showed up in my Life to be grateful for. Wow. That's cool.

I hadn't expected to notice anything different happening in my Life. Yet, there it was, Clear As Day... more nuances... more connexions... more insights... to be grateful for.

As I continued counting my blessings... it began occurring to me... it's one thing to think about what you're grateful for... it's a whole other thing to *feel* grateful. There is a remarkable difference between exploring gratitude with your mental body... versus delving into gratitude in your emotional nature. Your thinkery can easily get caught in the busy-ness of just checking stuff off the list. "Three things to be grateful for... right! Check... check... check. Done."

To give yourself the full-meal deal... you want to do some deeper delving around inside. To truly *feel* grateful. It makes a difference. When I first started experimenting with *feeling* grateful... I found I was a bit adrift. Great feelings of gratitude didn't exactly well up inside of me. I felt pretty flat... like cardboard. I knew I was grateful... but actually *feeling* grateful did not immediately come naturally.

I cast about inside for a time I felt grateful. Here's what popped up... I was about 9 years old... my dad picked me up from school that day. This didn't happen very often. He took me grocery shopping with him. As we were at the check-out stand... there in the midst of the impulse-buy candy aisle was a Bit-O-Honey candy bar. When I showed it to my dad... he bought it for me. Oh wow! This didn't happen very often, either. I have a clear memory of walking to our car across the hot parking lot savoring that Bit-O-Honey. I felt happily grateful. It was delish! He actually bought it for me! Thanks, Daddy.

Early in my process of exercising my gratitude muscle... recalling that moment became my inner go-to example of feeling grateful. When I couldn't quite conjure the grateful feeling... I'd remember that Bit-O-Honey moment and feel my happy 9 year old gratitude. Then I'd apply that feeling to my current gratefulness. Build those gratitude muscles. Exercise 'em. It works.

There is Grace in Gratitude.

Choosing to expose yourself to gratitude and appreciation leads you to focus on what *is* rather than fixating on what is not. Seeing, and appreciating, what I have moves me in a whole different direction. Away from only seeing what I don't have... and how much I want it. Away from how unfair it is that I don't have it... and what a drag my Life is.

Crossing the threshold into Appreciation, you open to the moment. You call the wisdom of the moment out to meet you. You say "Yes!" to The Great Possibility.

"How do I get there from here?" I want my Life to feel better. I want to awaken and develop my awareness. I want to feel better in my own skin. How do I do that?

Here, for your perusal... a review of The 3 Steps:

1. Listen to Your Thoughts

Attitude *IS* everything.

What are you telling yourself, day in & day out? What does your mental dialogue sound like? What "tone of voice" do you use with yourself?

You will develop your awareness as you change your caustic thoughts. Change your mind. Change your thoughts. Your life *will* change. Transform your harsh judgments... self-limiting beliefs... and pessimistic orientation. Don't let stinkin' thinkin' win.

2. Self-Kindness

Emotional Aerobics.

Exercise Self-Compassion. Self-Forgiveness. Self-Understanding. Give this gentle... yet profound... transformation an opportunity to unfold.

Rearrange your emotional corpuscles. Drop your conflict. Release the past. Forgive perceived slights. Forgive your self. Lasting transformation occurs as you honor yourself.

3. Appreciation

A Life-Transforming Force.

Unless you appreciate what you already have, little vibrant and new can come into your Life. As you say Thank You, you open the door in your own awareness for clarity, meaning, and growth to flow in.

When you know you are blessed, you are doubly blessed. Generate appreciation in your heart and in your mind. I am so grateful. I am so blessed. Be willing to work it. It's worth the effort. You're worth the effort.

Step 1 - Step 2 - Step 3. Rinse and Repeat.

Don't just take my word for it. Experiment within yourself. Stretch. Give yourself that quality of time and attentiveness. What happens when I…?

This being human occurs in a paradoxical universe. One minute, you're feeling pretty good… confident… on top of things. The next minute, you're consumed with doubt and anxiety… convinced you are messed up.

In this inner connect-the-dots journey we are each on… stories and pictures have an effective ability to reveal insight.

The following story is one of my faves... one of the best to confirm a striking Life truth.

A compelling Native American tale tells of a young brave's inner struggle as he prepares for his first vision quest. His anxiety grows as the day approaches. Nervous with both excitement and trepidation... one minute, he is sure he's going to have a meaningful vision. He will be a hero for his tribe. The next minute, he is sure nothing will happen. He will be a failure and let the tribe down.

The day before he is to leave on his quest... his doubt and fear ripping at him... the young brave seeks out his wise, old grandfather. "Help me, Grandfather. There are two vicious dogs battling inside me. One is certain that my quest will go well and I will return to our people with a bold vision. The other dog howls that I will fail in my quest and be a disappointment to the tribe. They are each fierce. Their fighting inside me is making me crazy! Help me, Grandfather. Tell me... which one is going to win?"

His grandfather quietly replies, "The one you feed."

And that's it.

The one you feed.

The one you give your attention to.

Be willing to invest in and care for yourself. Invest the time... the exercise... the practice... it takes to open to your own becoming. After decades of indulging in limiting beliefs and negative self-talk... your awareness has calcified into its current state. A state that may not be serving you as well as you'd like.

It's time to change channels. Tune your filter. Re-focus your lens. Dissolve those calcified deposits.

Game on.

This human instrument comes equipt with a fully-operational Capacity for Gratitude. You activate this feature as you remember you have it. As you give Gratitude your attention. Apply thought... and feeling energy... to what you appreciate about your Life and who you want to be.

> Look in the direction you want to go.
> Focus there.
> Drop any fixation on the poo.
> (Really... you *can* just drop it.)
>
> Notice the good stuff.
> Make the choice.
>
> Feed *that* dog.

Acknowledgments

With a warm heart, I acknowledge…

My awesome husband, Scott. Even after 37 years, you continue to delight me with your keen insight, your playful laughter, and your loving encouragement and support.

Our dear friend, Joy Utz, C.F.o.F. Our very own Certified Facilitator of Fun. Mahalo for you… and for your kind generosity and attentive, caring ways.

Rita Leiphart, C.C.H. Your talent and artistry helped me actually birth Holy Wow! after a ridiculously long gestation.

Our son, Isaiah. Oh, how you grace my Life just by being your fine self.

I am blessed beyond measure by the many gifts of insight and connexion that have come my way… thanks to the extraordinary friends and fellow humans who have touched my Life.

I warmly thank Karen Myer and Rev. Dr. Maureen Hoyt who both kindly read the *Volume I* manuscript… making sure the T's were crossed and the I's were dotted.

You hold this book in your hands right now thanks to the generosity of spirit and skillful coaching of Amy Collins. A Big Thanks to Amy. Period. And more appreciation to Amy for recommending my ideal editors, Pam Cangioli and Kim Jace, as well as my very talented cover designer, Mila… Miladinka Milic. Pam Cangioli led me to Ghislain Viau who has done an excellent job as my interior book designer. Stephanie Barko provided her expertise as my literary publicist. Keri-Rae Barnum, Amy Collin's Marketing Director, gets a big shout out for helping me push the right buttons to actually Publish!

To each of you for the part you played in bringing *Holy Wow!* into being… Mahalo Plenty!

Acknowledging that you, kind Reader, might be interested in connecting with any of these talented and very helpful individuals… here are their websites:

Rita Leiphart – www.districthypnosis.com
Rev. Dr. Maureen Hoyt – www.drmaureenhoyt.com
Amy Collins – www.newshelves.com
Pam Cangioli – www.proofedtoperfection.com
Miladinka Milic – www.milagraphicartist.com
Ghislain Viau – www.creativepublishingdesign.com
Stephanie Barko – www.stephaniebarko.com

About The Author

Blessed to share the rich gifts of mindfulness, Dana has been teaching others to meditate for over 40 years. Recognizing we are Spirit living a human experience, she is fascinated by the rich tapestry of Life… and the many gifts and possibilities available to every human.

It is Dana's delight to play the temple gongs, bells and tingsha that grace her guided meditations. She recognizes this as "a past Life thing." As Dana says… "The resonant tones of the gongs take you places mere words could never find."

She follows her own advice to "choose to be amused." And finds great pleasure in being a wordsmith. As an ordained transdenominational minister, Dana is a Celebrationist, creating Weddings, Memorial Services, and other Life-enhancing ceremony and ritual

Dana and her husband, Scott, live in Kona, Hawaii, ever in awe of the miraculous sunsets.

Holy Wow! Volume I is Dana's first book.

Holy Wow! Volume II

Hello… this is your Team Interpretorium Activities Director here, with the continuing imprint of your Orientation Guidebook.

Holy Wow! Volume II
is Team Interpretorium's Earth Operative Manual.

Insightful and quirky… you'll find some real juicy stuff.

As your journey into personhood continues to unfold… *Holy Wow! Volume II* offers much more to explore. Arranging your cognitive essence, and activating your Incarnant Paraphernalia… you are primed to cross The Threshold into that Grand and Glorious MultiPlex Adventure… Incarnating Human on Planet Earth.

Holy Wow! Volume II = an excellent travel companion on your Awakening Awareness Safari. There are invigorating elements waiting for you to discover in *Volume II*. As you incarnate into this electrifying era in human development… Extreme *Consciousness* Sport is in full swing! The evolution of human awareness is quickening! I know you are jazzed to show up on Earth for this exhilarating opportunity!

Volume II holds insights into The 7 Kingdom Format of Planetary Life… as well as the ever-evolving Spectrum of

Human Awareness. This Spectrum evolves from Instinct to Intellect… Intellect to Intuition… Intuition to Inspiration. And wrapped in your human suit… you'll be there! As Human Awareness moves beyond the limitations of Instinct and Intellect. You're on site to experience humankind's progression into the vast, clear realizations of Intuition and Inspiration.

Perusing the *Volume II* prospectus, I hear you wondering… what *is* the HazMat Variety Show? Will I be affected by it? Well, yes… chances are very likely you will be. These corrosive physical substances… and toxic emotional tendencies… deeply influence the lives of Earthtone humans.

Volume II continues exploring the Realm of Eternal Love… with robust Life-revelations and growing awareness of The Love That Heals. You will find insight into the gift of forgiveness… the gift of releasing yourself from hurt and anger.

A Recent Returnee joins us in *Volume II*… sharing insight and perceptions gleaned from her most recent Planet Earth incarnation. She includes insightful commentary and valuable suggestions on parenting with loving awareness.

"Sexness: Friend or Foe?" *Volume II* presents uplifting Tantric enhancements within the vast and wide realms of human sexuality. Sexness… ever humanity's dilemma. Ever humanity's delight. You won't want to miss that!

Equipt with enriching parenting skills + embracing the grace of your sexuality = profound impact on how gratifying… how luminous… your upcoming human incarnation will be.

You already know Planet Earth is a prime destination resort… one of our most popular incarnant locales. In *Volume II* you are encouraged to visit Realizmotron's Destination Dioramas. There you will experience the weather… the what… and the wherefores… of many different neighborhoods, terrains, and localities.

Holy Wow! Volume II is ripe with insight components galore. "Mind-blowing," as the locals say. These insights are *yours*. To recall. Embrace. Activate. To make your own. As you flourish in the realm of Spirit having a human experience. Good times.

Soon coming your way!
Holy Wow! Volume II

Insight abounds. And a few good laughs.
Keys to manage fear, anxiety and distress.
The unexpected benefits of Gratitude and Forgiveness.

What role do you play in this remarkable Life?
Let go of self-imposed limitations.
And what's Love got to do with it?

The handbook for human awareness waking up.
Empower your Life.

Maylaigh.com/Danas-Book
Maylaigh.com/Maylaigh-Media
Facebook @revdanastclaire
Goodreads @Dana St. Claire

www.ingramcontent.com/pod-product-compliance
Lightning Source LLC
Chambersburg PA
CBHW031104080526
44587CB00011B/821